The Prosody of the Tudor Interlude

J. E. BERNARD, JR.

ARCHON BOOKS
1969

Reprinted 1969 with permission of Yale University Press
in an unaltered and unabridged edition

[*Yale Studies in English, Vol. 90*]

SBN: 208 00782 2
Library of Congress Catalog Card Number: 69-15677
Printed in the United States of America

To C. B. T.

e come in voce voce si discerne . . .

—*Div. Comm.* III. viii. 17.

CONTENTS

PREFACE

The seventy-odd interludes written between 1497 and 1593 are characterized by a variety of verse forms whose variation is more often extended to the scheme of rimes than to the length of single lines. The metrics fall into three main groups: couplets bearing from two to seven linear stresses, rime couée of six and eight lines, and ballad measures of from four to eight lines.

The interludes are considered one by one, each with a tabulation of its metrical nature. The results of an endeavor to link changes in rime scheme with internal changes in the plays are more in the style of observations than conclusions, but from the history of the metres in the course of the century the following may be deduced:

1. The verse of the Tudor interlude must not be merely condemned by our present syllabic criteria as doggerel.
2. It was indigenous to England and had no connexion with Continental poetics.
3. The playwrights were concerned with varying their verse in accord with what took place in the drama.
4. In general, their concern emphasized the contrast between two systems; for example, virtue and serious passages were often presented in ballad measures, and vice and frolicsome passages in rime couée.
5. All complicated measures were laid aside with the advent of prose and blank verse about 1588.
6. Evidence is strengthened in favor of the suggested authorship of certain plays: *Gentleness and Nobility, Jacob and Esau, Respublica, Jack Juggler.*
7. Evidence is weakened in favor of the suggested authorship of certain plays: *Godly Queen Hester, Calisto and Melibea, Thersites.*

This study was originally presented to the faculty of Yale University by way of candidacy for the degree of Doctor of Philosophy, and to four of its members is due whatever merit may attach to the following pages. The work was conceived at the suggestion of Mr. Brooke and was fostered under his hand; Mr. Berdan, Mr. Witherspoon, and Mr. Warren Smith have gone over the text and have offered invaluable assistance in its final preparation.

BIBLIOGRAPHICAL ABBREVIATIONS

The works in this list are referred to only by the author's surname.

Adams, J. Q. *Chief Pre-Shakespearean Dramas.* Cambridge (Mass.), 1924.

Berdan, J. M. *Early Tudor Poetry 1485-1547.* New York, 1931.

Bond, R. W. *Early Plays from the Italian.* Oxford, 1911.

Bradner, L. "A Test for Udall's Authorship." *Modern Language Notes* (1927), xlii. 378-380.

Brandl, A. "Quellen des weltlichen Dramas in England vor Shakespeare." *Quellen und Forschungen* (1898), lxxx.

Brooke, C. F. T. *The Tudor Drama.* Boston, 1911.

Eckhardt, E. *Das englische Drama im Zeitalter der Reformation und der Hochrenaissance.* 2 vols. Berlin, 1928.

Henderson, T. F. *Scottish Vernacular Literature.* London, 1898.

Hendren, J. W. *A Study of Ballad Rhythm with Special Reference to Ballad Music.* Princeton (N. J.), 1936.

Macdonald, J. F. "The Use of Prose in English Drama before Shakespeare." *University of Toronto Quarterly* (1933), ii. 465-481.

Manly, J. M. *Specimens of the Pre-Shakespearean Drama.* 2 vols. Boston, 1900.

Patterson, W. F. *Three Centuries of French Poetic Theory.* 2 vols. Ann Arbor (Mich.), 1935.

Ramsay, R. L. *Magnificence: a Moral Play, by John Skelton.* London, 1908.

Reyher, P. *Essai sur le doggerel.* Bordeaux, 1909.

Saintsbury, G. E. B. *History of English Prosody.* 3 vols. London, 1906-10.

Schipper, J. *Englische Metrik.* 3 vols. Bonn, 1888.

Schröer, A. "'A comedy concernynge thre lawes' von Johan Bale." *Anglia* (1882), v. 238-264.

Whiting, B. J. *Proverbs in the Earlier English Drama.* Cambridge (Mass.), 1938.

Young, G. *An English Prosody on Inductive Lines.* Cambridge, 1928.

THE PROSODY OF THE TUDOR INTERLUDE

In a prosodic consideration of the verse in which the interludes were written, an attempt to reduce to a science unscientific versification, one must necessarily be content with outlines. Interludes were primarily folk-drama, and the verse which more or less confined their lines was a secondary consideration. Prosody as the science of versification presupposes an attempt at poetic contour by the writer in presenting his subject as poetry.[1] Those who produced the interludes, on the other hand, did not for a moment think to write poetry. They were writing living drama which was to be acted, spoken, heard, and received; the form in which this drama was cast was, as if by accident, that of verse. The form of the drama coincided with that of verse; there was no further *rapprochement*, certainly no wedding of poetic thought to poetic form.[2] Indeed, for the student to approach poetically, i.e. prosodically, what was assuredly intended only for acting drama might seem to be putting the shoe on the wrong foot; but the diversity of metrical form is so rich as to persuade him that a bilateral consideration is not out of place.

Prosody as a study of the construction of verse is as a rule concerned with the structure of single lines, for in most cases the pattern of a single line, however it may be internally varied, is that of the poem. In such cases the interest is centred in the individual line: in its syllabication, in its stresses, accents, pauses, cæsuras, in its rhythmic variety, and in the various details that go toward making it poetic in

[1] L. Abercrombie, *The Theory of Poetry* (New York, 1926); J. B. Mayor, *Chapters on English Metre* (London, 1901); T. S. Omond, *English Metrists* (Oxford, 1927). For a discussion and critical appraisal of the many modern works on English prosody, see P. Barkas, *A Critique of Modern English Prosody (1880-1930)* (Halle [Saale], 1934). A selected bibliography is printed on pp. 10-1.

[2] A. W. Reed, *The Beginnings of the English Secular and Romantic Drama* (London, 1922), p. 10, has pointed out a singular exception to this statement of general truth. The lines occur in Medwall's *Nature* (43-49).

outline as the ideas go toward making it poetic in content.[3] But just as the authors of the interludes had no concern with poetical content, neither had they any concern with poetic outline as far as individual lines were considered. The line was a matter of little importance to them. That it should embrace now eight syllables, now thirty-eight, did not challenge their sense of form.[4] The line was an atom and nothing more, and no account was taken of the fact that the atom might itself have strict form, that it might be composed of tinier particles charged with complexes of factual, rhythmic, or melodic association.

The singleness of the dramatic eye which John Heywood and the other writers of interludes possessed thus permitted nearly all focus to be concentrated on groups of lines. Now, prosody is concerned primarily with the single line—as most books on the subject devote nine-tenths of their attention to the same—and this is influenced by the element of poetical content.[5] In the case of the interludes with the general absence of such interest, the result is that all attention must be brought to bear on groups of lines. Usually these lines are grouped in pairs, providing a minimum of prosodic interest as well as a minimum of effort in the writing. Very often, however, the lines are grouped stanzaically. The outcome is that the corpus of interludes provides a heterogeneous wealth of verse-forms, a chaos into which it is possible to bring a certain amount of order.

When one brings order to this chaos, it must not be brought in the Procrustean manner. One cannot take a mathematical yardstick to every line, for the lines are not constituted to withstand drastic means of mensuration. The dramatists had comparatively little regard for the individual line beyond its integrity. This investigation of the prosody

[3] M. A. Bayfield, *Shakespeare's Versification* (Cambridge, 1920), especially pp. 11-25.

[4] The most flagrant case is to be found in *The Three Ladies of London*, the last line on p. 210 of the text containing forty syllables. *Damon and Pythias* similarly tags with rime the twenty-fifth syllable in line 313. See pp. 176 and 133.

[5] P. Verrier, *Principes de la métrique anglaise* (Paris, 1909. 3 vols.), i. 263-342.

which obtains in the interludes therefore endeavors as closely as possible to approach the aspect of versification as it was approached by those who wrote the verses. Their interest was in the grouping of the lines, the evidence indicates, and it is with such grouping that this study is concerned. Some apology is necessary in diverting the attention from the main prosodic stream to one of its by-waters, but such diversion is in this case imperative. The lines cannot all be scanned; few in fact will submit to the straitjackets of iamb and anapæst.[6] They were not written to be iambic or anapæstic but to be parts of a whole.

The survey thus becomes primarily a study in rime,[7] for by this means the lines are linked. In so discussing the versification of the interludes, i.e. strophically, there must be found a means of noting the size of the lines which constitute the stanzas. From the very beginning, the length of the lines varied within wide syllabic limits, and the only common denominator is to be found in the number of stresses which the lines contain. Only too often is the reader's ingenuity taxed to provide a satisfactory modulus. The inconsistency of the number of syllables, accents, and the various other elements by which one might hope to get a satisfactory prosodic hold on the lines forces one to conclude that the only proper method of consideration is by means of beats or stresses. The whole subject will therefore be presented as a study in stress and rime: they will be the medium through which the results will be derived.

All factors point to this method of consideration as fitting. Even those plays now extant in holograph[8] betray such unevenness of versification that one cannot presume the interludes to have been written by students of theses and arses. Nor can one blame the printers for taking liberties with the text. Some of the printing is indeed bad, amounting even

[6] The striking exception to this rule is the work of George Gascoigne, himself in 1575 the author of the earliest modern treatise on English prosody. See below, p. 8, n. 30; p. 12, n. 47.

[7] G. Young, *An English Prosody on Inductive Lines* (Cambridge, 1928), pp. 105-10.

[8] *Respublica, King John, Witty and Witless.*

to inversions of words to mutilate an accurately followed scheme;[9] but the typesetters cannot be charged with corrupting an original worthy of the mediæval Latinists.[10]

To generalize, the first writers of the interludes were men of the court circle, often musicians as well.[11] Of the *parvenu* Tudor aristocracy they made a comparate part; their traditions and their education were English, free from foreign sophistication. The drama with which they were familiar was for the most part that indigenous to English soil, the influence of the *quattrocento* in Italy not yet having been experienced, and the *sotties* of the French stage affecting the content of only a handful of plays.[12] The sources for the form of the interludes were to be discovered in the moralities from which they grew, developments of the church-drama which employed complicated verse-forms.[13]

The conditions under which the interludes were written would further condone the "lax" approach of the authors to a rigid versification. The plays were composed by men whose vocations were in other fields. Some were musicians, some were clergymen, some were strolling players; none were vocational poets.[14] The interludes were written to grace a

[9] *Fulgens and Lucres*, text, II. 104, 109.

[10] See pp. 102, 193-5.

[11] John Heywood, John Redford, Richard Edwards.

[12] *Respublica, A Satire of the Three Estates* (at Edinburgh), *Magnificence*, and the plays of John Bale. See, however, K. Young, "The Influence of French Farce upon the Plays of John Heywood," *Modern Philology* (1904), ii. 97-124.

[13] E. Eckhardt, *Das englische Drama im Zeitalter der Reformation und der Hochrenaissance* (Berlin, 1928. 2 vols.), i. 38; M. D. Fort, "The Metres of the Brome and Chester Abraham and Isaac plays," *Publications of the Modern Language Association* (1926), xli. 832-9; H. Meier, *Die Strophenform in den englischen Mysterienspielen* (Freiburg, 1921); R. L. Ramsay, *Magnificence: a Moral Play by John Skelton* (London, 1908), pp. cxxxiv-cxl, cxliv-cxlv; P. Reyher, *Essai sur le doggerel* (Bordeaux, 1909), pp. 42-51; G. Saintsbury, *History of English Prosody* (London, 1906-10. 3 vols.), i. 203-17; J. Schipper, *Englische Metrik* (Bonn, 1888. 3 vols.), i. 218-31.

[14] The poetical work of Heywood, Edwards, and Gascoigne scarcely entitles them to be considered "professional," so to speak, in the sense of Michael Drayton or Edmund Spenser.

particular occasion, originally the interim between two halves of a banquet,[15] and, having perhaps been put on by children, then to be discarded.[16] Such conditions are not conducive to the production of good poetry, particularly when the verses are not intended to be considered as poetry at all. The ways by which the writers drew near the subject of poetry were not those by which we, affected as we are by the academic tradition which has been crescent for three hundred years,[17] are wont to travel.

In going on to a study of the prosody, these things must be kept in mind, with one's ear to be the final judge. The results of such a judgment naturally cannot be claimed inexpugnable, but they can be expected to show, within the average range of fallibility, the trend of dramatic verse-making in the course of the century. Another reader will doubtless achieve results which vary statistically from those which follow, but the larger contours cannot fail to make themselves evident, and it is this which inspires this study.

It is necessary for the modern reader to come to the subject of rime with an open ear. Those who wrote the interludes so often made assonance and ocular rime take the place of mere rime that separation is valueless. With the realization that four centuries ago words were not pronounced as they are today,[18] that vowels possessed a "brogue" which the metro-

[15] See *Fulgens and Lucres*, text, pp. xxi-xxii.

[16] See p. 192, and H. N. Hillebrand, *The Child Actors* (Urbana [Ill.], 1926), pp. 57-150, 253-88.

[17] In the last generation, however, grown gibbous; e.g. see T. S. Eliot, "Introduction" to Marianne Moore, *Selected Poems* (New York, 1935); R. P. Blackmur, *The Double Agent* (New York, 1935), pp. 163-4.

[18] C. Davies, *English Pronunciation from the Fifteenth to the Eighteenth Century* (London, 1934); A. J. Ellis, *Early English Pronunciation* (Edinburgh, 1869-89. 5 vols.), iii. 877-996; S. Lanier, *Shakespeare and his Forerunners* (New York, 1902. 2 vols.), i. 271-93; W. Viëtor, *A Shakespeare Phonology* (Marburg, 1906. 2 vols.), i.; R. E. Zachrisson, "The English Pronunciation at Shakespeare's Time as Taught by William Bullokar [1580]," *Skrifter Utgivna av Kungl. Humanistiska Vetenkaps-Samfundet* (Uppsala, 1927), xxii. 60-243.

politan language has lost, one must come prepared to deal liberally with the vagaries of versification.[19]

The present survey includes the seventy-odd interludes which appeared between 1497 and 1593, the date of *Summer's Last Will and Testament,* the point of climax of this form of drama. Sophistication from the professional drama had so entered into its fibre that the interlude was no longer worthy of the name. As the dates stand, they embrace virtually the whole of the sixteenth century as well as the significant folk-drama, defining precisely the time-limits of the work in hand.

The tabulations which follow have been made with the foregoing principles in view. The texts have been selected for their general utility, and numbers for the lines have been provided when necessary. Since the order of presentation is intended to be chronological, the dates given are the earliest to which the plays can conveniently be assigned.[20] Alliteration and various other characteristics of the verse in question are noted. Dissyllabic and trisyllabic rime are more specific terms than feminine rime, which places the accent generally on the syllable next to the last. This provides a tapering off, a prosodic luxuriousness foreign to everything else in the interludes. So often, indeed, does the accent rise in the case of double rimes that the opposite effect is produced, and the listener has the feeling of force redoubled.[21]

Since the prosody of the drama is separate from that of poetry for the reasons cited above, it has been deemed neces-

[19] Rime, for example, is never disturbed by the presence of a foreign *s* in the plural. *D* and *th, k* and *t, y* and *ie* are among the most usual assonances, the last pair being particularly cherished. See Young, pp. 108-9. For slipshod rimes *Lusty Juventus* and *King Darius* might be placed by the side of *Damon and Pythias* and *The Three Ladies of London.*

[20] Very often based on conjecture alone. Eckhardt (op. cit.) has generally been used for this purpose as the most recent epitome of the interludes, supplemented by B. J. Whiting, *Proverbs in the Earlier English Drama* (Cambridge [Mass.], 1938).

[21] *Seven, heaven,* and similar words are considered as the monosyllables they were pronounced, nor can an unaccented *-d* or *-ed* from the preterite be expected to create a double rime.

sary to omit from this survey the songs which occur in the interludes. The ideals which gave rise to their versification are different, and it often bears no relation to the versification of the play as a whole. They make use of continental devices stemming from the *poétrie* of France[22] and the mediæval verse-forms.[23] Change and development in their form is of no consequence in the study of dramatic prosody, and the lyric measures are better let severely alone than allowed to intrude upon a study of this kind.[24]

Identical rime had the same debilitating effect on verse as verse as it has today, remote from the *rime riche* that was the ideal of Guillaume de Machaut. Redundant rime is considered to be the extravasation of rime beyond the confines of its due group—stanza or couplet—except in the case of rime royal, whose stanzas may be linked by this means. In this case alone leakage becomes linkage.[25]

The names of stanzas of more than four lines have occasionally been borrowed from the French, but no more than this is intended. Neuvain, for example, is herein used to designate only the stanza of nine lines couées and has no connexion with the French form.[26]

The nomenclature of the various metres encountered must be arbitrary.[27] The terms two-stress, four-stress, etc. are rather too cumbersome in English to warrant reiteration for the course of this project, and although their accuracy is unquestioned and even preferable to that of other terms, it is advisable to use the more familiar dimeter, tetrameter, etc.

[22] W. F. Patterson, *Three Centuries of French Poetic Theory* (Ann Arbor [Mich.], 1935. 2 vols.), i. 13-96.

[23] See pp. 193-5.

[24] The number of lines set down in the tables following will therefore not include those contained in the songs.

[25] The ballad-eight or Monk's Tale stanza is a case of two linked quatrains, but the term linkage will be reserved for stanzas of rime royal.

[26] Riming ababbcdcd.

[27] Terms used in the designation of the various forms will be found explained in the treatises of G. Saintsbury, *Historical Manual of English Prosody* (London, 1910), and L. Untermeyer, *The Forms of Poetry* (New York, 1936).

in their stead.[28] For the purposes of the discussion, then, each foot will consist of a stressed syllable and other unstressed syllables *quantum sufficiat*. It will not, as in later verse, be an inflexible unit, variation in which is a matter for comment, but merely the most convenient name by which may be designated the entire wave of rhythm, crest and trough.[29]

There is no need to define the stanza-forms to be met; they have long been familiar. They fall into three groups: the couplet, the ballad measures, and the waist-and-tailed schemes of rime couée. The couplet may have from two to seven beats; in poulter's measure the second half is usually two syllables longer than the first.[30] For the rest, the tumbling verse of King James and the long fourteeners ride along yoked in pairs.

The ballad measures begin with four lines riming alternately.[31] That of six lines employs the scheme ababcc,[32]

[28] The same is true of the correct but unfamiliar designations of Sir George Young. Cinquepace (op. cit., pp. 10-104) is at least as good a word as pentameter, and cantilever verse (pp. 111-2) is an admirable way of referring to the light line of four stresses with the central cæsura.

[29] The words tetrameter, pentameter, etc. are intended for the equivalent of four or five monopodies. The use of these terms after the Greek manner, in which e.g. tetrameter comes to signify a verse of four dipodies, or eight stresses (J. Ruskin, *Elements of English Prosody*. [London, 1880]), will find no application here.

[30] Schipper, i. 253-7, ii. 429, 557, etc. The term of Gascoigne (*Works*, ed. J. W. Cunliffe [Cambridge, 1907-10. 2 vols.]; i. 472) finds little employment in the interlude before its appearance in *Certain Notes of Instruction Concerning the Making of Verse or Rime in English* (1575), par. 14. See also Saintsbury, i. 310-1.

[31] K. Brunner, "Zum Balladenrhythmus," *Archiv für das Studium der neueren Sprachen* (1920), cxl. 259-61; J. W. Hendren, *A Study of Ballad Rhythm with Special Reference to Ballad Music*, p. 99 (Princeton [N. J.], 1936); T. Maynard, *The Connection between the Ballade, Chaucer's Adaptation of it, Rime Royal, and the Spenserian Stanza* (Washington [D. C.], 1934); L. Pound, "The Uniformity of the Ballad Style," *Modern Language Notes* (1920), xxxv. 217-22; G. R. Stewart jr., "The Meter of the Popular Ballad," *Publications of the Modern Language Association* (1925), xl. 933-62.

[32] The romance-six.

that of seven lines is the rime royal, ababbcc, and the eight-line strophe rimes ababbcbc.[33] Although rime royal belongs particularly to seven lines of iambic pentameter riming as above, the term will here be used without reference to the individual line and will signify merely that the rimes are thus distributed. Analogously the other designations will take no account of syllables but refer only to the rime pattern.

Rime couée occurs usually in groups of six or eight lines, to be called sixain coué and octave couée respectively. There are instances in which the rime in the tail is carried on to produce a stanza of nine, twelve, or even eighteen lines,[34] and there are cases in some of the more roughly hewn interludes in which extra triplets are left unattached.[35] These must be recognized as parts of the system of rime couée.

There was also a curious revival of the old alliterative verse—if it can be said ever to have died—which escapes all attempts to transfix it.[36] It cannot be scanned; one can merely point it out in places where it becomes apparent. The rhythm of such verse is stressed and accentual, bearing the listener along as if from crest to crest of a strong surge, and there is herein probably to be found the source for stress as the chief metrical element in the single line.[37] It was the combination of the alliterative system of beats, long surviving alliteration as its *raison d'être*, with the schemes of rime

[33] The stanza of Geoffrey Chaucer's *Monk's Tale*. It is also the scheme of the French *huitain*; see p. 7, n. 26.

[34] Especially in *Nature, The World and the Child*, and *Godly Queen Hester*.

[35] *The Four Elements, Hickscorner*.

[36] See below, p. 203, and G. Saintsbury, *Manual of English Prosody* (London, 1910), pp. 48, 165. Reyher, p. 39, discusses the effect of the appearance in 1550 and 1560 of two editions of *Piers Plowman*; see also A. Schröer, "'A comedy concernynge thre lawes' von Johan Bale," *Anglia* (1882), v. 240. For a complete discussion of the poetical background, see J. P. Oakden, *Alliterative Poetry in Middle English* (Manchester, 1930-5. 2 vols.).

[37] K. Luick, "Zur Metrik der mittelenglischen reimend-alliterierenden Dichtung," *Anglia* (1889), xii. 437-53; W. W. Skeat, "An Essay on Alliterative Poetry," *Bishop Percy's Folio Manuscript*, ed. J. W. Hales and F. J. Furnivall (London, 1867-8. 3 vols.), iii. pp. xi-xliv.

inherited from the morality plays, that the outward form of the Tudor interlude was originally evolved.

The work that has already been done on the prosody of the interludes[38] deserves a note of comment before going on to an individual discussion. They are usually dismissed with a word like doggerel,[39] occasionally expanded to Skeltonic doggerel.[40] A few of the more important have merited separate discussion as far as a cataloguing of their rime schemes,[41] but in general little attempt has been made to unravel the various metrical skeins. The dictum of George Saintsbury that this drama was prosodic anarchy and that it contained "doggerel of all kinds" has gone unchallenged. Of course it does contain doggerel of all kinds, but to dismiss

[38] R. W. Bond, *Early Plays from the Italian* (Oxford, 1911), pp. lxxx-xc, civ-cvii; A. Brandl, "Quellen des weltlichen Dramas in England vor Shakespeare," *Quellen und Forschungen* (1898), lxxx. pp. xxxvii-cxviii; W. Creizenach, *Geschichte des neueren Dramas* (Halle, 1893-1915. 5 vols.), iii. 504-5; J. P. Dabney, *The Musical Basis of Verse* (New York, 1901), p. 198; Eckhardt, i. 38; E. E. Jones, *John Bale's Drama God's Promises* (Erlangen, 1909), pp. xvi-xix; Ramsay, pp. li-lxxi, cxxxiv-cxlvii; Reyher, pp. 42-66; Saintsbury, i. 335-43; Schröer, pp. 238-64; Schipper, i. 231-42, 255-7, 291-3.

[39] . . . Le sens très vague de mauvaise poésie, de méchants vers, faux ou boiteux faits à la diable et dépourvus d'harmonie. Il [doggerel] désigne souvent des vers difficiles ou impossibles à scander. Les uns sont des épaves de l'ancienne versification anglo-saxonne; les autres résultent d'un mélange, d'un 'croisement,' ou d'un conflit de deux systèmes prosodiques; d'autres encore sont dus au manque d'oreille ou à la négligence de quelque rimailleur; d'autres enfin ont été faits à dessein, avec une intention comique, et constituent un véritable crime de lèse-versification avec préméditation. Ces vers, ces prétendus vers, sont presque toujours rimés: certains renferment quelques pieds, ce qui, à la lecture, donne l'impression passagère d'un rhythme, d'autant mieux qu'ils se trouvent souvent mêlés à des vers réguliers et sont donnés par leurs auteurs comme des vers; mais on ne peut franchement pas les considérer comme tels. Et cependant ce ne sont pas, à strictement parler, des lignes de prose: ils tiennent donc à la fois du vers et de la prose, sont quelque chose d'intermédiaire entre les deux, un produit hybride et bâtard de l'un et de l'autre. [Reyher, pp. 106-7.]

[40] Bond, p. lxxxi; Reyher, pp. 26-36.

[41] *The Four Elements, Magnificence.*

it so is inadequate. Conscious cerebral effort is always connected with the sustained production of lines which rime not only by two but in alternation, from which grow the more complicated structures.

In treating this kind of subject cavilling is possible at every turn of the way. The nomenclature may be thought too inaccurate,[42] the elements of accent, time, pitch, stress, and address insufficiently reduced to the physiological and physical bases which can split a second into a hundred identical parts,[43] and the very notion of applying to poetry any prosodic measurement whatever may be deemed meat too strong for a queasy stomach.[44] Such demurrers are occasionally necessary to prevent carelessness in the judicious appreciation of poetry æsthetically,[45] but in dealing with the Tudor interludes squeamishness is out of place. All subtleties of notation, all delicate attempts to connect this dramatic poetry with music[46] must be put behind in an endeavor to catch the sweep

[42] M. W. Croll, "Music and Metrics: a Reconsideration," *Studies in Philology* (1923), xx. 388-94.

[43] "A Canon for English Verse," *Times Literary Supplement* (1925), xxiv. 584, 600, 619, 639, 656, 675, 719, 739, 756, 772, 812, 835 (Contributions by J. P. Postgate, A. Y. Campbell, T. S. Moore, and others); H. Lanz, "The Physical Basis of Rime," *Publications of the Modern Language Association* (1926), xli. 1011-23; W. L. Schramm, *Approaches to a Science of English Verse* (Iowa City [Ia.], 1935); A. L. F. Snell, "An Objective Study of Syllabic Quantity in English Verse," *Publications of the Modern Language Association* (1919), xxxiv. 416-35; H. P. Thieme, "Rhythm," *Mélanges d'histoire littéraire générale et comparée offerts à Fernand Baldensperger* (Paris, 1930), pp. 275-83; C. E. Whitmore, "A Proposed Compromise in Metrics," *Publications of the Modern Language Association* (1926), xli. 1024-43.

[44] H. Monroe, "A Word about Prosody," *Poetry* (1925), xxvii. 149-53.

[45] D. W. Prall, *Æsthetic Analysis* (New York, 1936), pp. 93-134.

[46] R. Bridges, "A Letter to a Musician on English Prosody," *Musical Antiquary* (Oct. 1909), i. 15-29; O. Goldsmith, "Versification." (Essay 18.) *The Miscellaneous Works of Oliver Goldsmith*, ed. D. Masson (London, 1928), pp. 339-41; S. Lanier, *The Science of English Verse* (New York, 1909); E. Sapir, "The Musical Founda-

and swing of verse that is intended to carry the listener along, not to titillate his softer emotions. In general, brave and brutal was the manner of its construction, and rugged practice yielded to no contemplative theorizing. Five works on prosody appeared during the age of the interlude and were ignored.[47] True, this form of the drama has nearly run its course by their time, but so great is the contrast between the work of Gascoigne in his interlude and that of his contemporaries that one instantly recognizes *The Glass of Government* as a step-child.

Only with these various things in mind is it possible to approach the question of versification in the Tudor interlude.[48] The characteristics of its verse and the application of these characteristics to the material of the play are the foci of this study; and though the figure to which they give

tions of Verse," *Journal of English and Germanic Philology* (1921), xx. 213-28; G. R. Stewart jr., "The Iambic-Trochaic Theory in Relation to Musical Notation of Verse," *Journal of English and Germanic Philology* (1925), xxiv. 61-71.

[47] See G. G. Smith, *Elizabethan Critical Essays* (Oxford, 1904. 2 vols.). The treatises were:

1575. George Gascoigne, *Certain Notes of Instruction Concerning the Making of Verse or Rime in English.* (Ibid., i. 46-57.)

1582. Richard Stanyhurst, "Too thee Learned Reader," prefatory to *Thee First Foure Bookes of Virgil his Aeneis.* (Ibid., i. 136-47.)

1584. King James VI., "*Ane Schort Treatise Conteining some Reulis and Cautelis to be Observit and Eschewit in Scottis Poesie.*" (Ibid., i. 208-25.)

1586. William Webbe, *A Discourse of English Poetry.* (Ibid., i. 226-302.)

1589. George Puttenham, *The Art of English Poesy.* (Ibid., ii. 3-193; see also the edition of G. D. Willcox and A. Walker [Cambridge, 1936], pp. lxiv-lxxiii.)

For a discussion of the above essays, see Smith, loc. cit., pp. xlvi-lx. Fortunately, too, the whole question of quantitative scansion does not enter into the metrics of the interludes. See also Schipper, ii. 223-5.

[48] For a parallel study of Shakespeare's versification, with a presentation of the problems involved, see E. K. Chambers, *William Shakespeare* (Oxford, 1930. 2 vols.), ii. 397-408.

substance is elliptic in contour, one can discern the moderately smooth prosodic curve which embraces the century of interludes.[49]

[49] Since no antiquarian purpose can be served in this type of project by preserving the antique spelling, the orthography has almost invariably been modernized with a view to simplicity and the elimination of unnecessary hazards. Titles have similarly been abbreviated and all things done that can assist in delineating most sharply the outlines of an obscure entropy.

The summaries make use of a normalized diction, but variants cannot conveniently be kept from the commentary. A list of terms which are for this use synonymous is therefore appended here:

Light: anapæstic.

Heavy: iambic.

Couplets: closed rime, immediate rime, consecutive rime.

Quatrains: open rime, alternate rime, cross-rime.

Rime couée: tail-rime, waist-and-tail rime, rime doggerel, Sir Thopas stanza.

Tetrameter couplets: cantilever verse, tumbling verse, dramatic doggerel, long doggerel.

Dimeter couplets: Skeltonics, Skeltonic doggerel, short doggerel, rimed hemistichs, half-line couplets.

Pentameter: cinquepace.

Hexameter: Alexandrine.

Heptameter: septenary, fourteener.

Ballad-six: hexastich, romance-six.

Rime royal: Chaucerian stanza, heptastich.

Ballad-eight: Monk's Tale stanza, octastich.

Wheel: burden, *frons*, *membrum*.

Tail: bob, *cauda*, *differentia*, etc. See also p. 7, n. 27; Hendren, pp. 174-5.

I. Interludium de Clerico et Puella

Text: W. Heuser, ed., *Anglia* (1907), xxx. 307-309.
Date: 1300.[1]
Rhythm: heavy.
Prevailing metre: tetrameter couplets.

Lines:	84	%
Redundant rime:[2]	1	1.2
Rime lacking:[2]	1	1.2
Tetrameter couplets:	84	100.

As happy prologue to the imperial age of the interlude, the *Interludium de Clerico et Puella* takes on an historical significance. Earlier by a hundred years than the first of the true interludes, it is a Middle English introduction, already in the rimed line of four stresses, to the future. It could be found in the middle of the sixteenth century, other things being equal, and excite no comment, for its versification parallels that of a host of similar folk plays. The proportions of the various prosodic quirks noted above are those of the interludes which follow. Alliteration has not yet come to this style of writing, and one must notice that the metre is heavy or iambic, that it does not go rollicking off on the anapæsts that were to alleviate the pietistic atmosphere. When it has been called typical of the true interludes, one has summed it up—an anticipation of those which characterize the latter half of the century.

[1] Text, p. 306.

[2] When these aberrations from the conscious scheme of the playwright occur, they will generally not be subtracted from the number of lines listed as of a specific kind. Only when they appear in a body will they be excluded from the group. In the present case, for example, although there are by actual count but 82 lines of rimed tetrameter, the scheme is intended to carry through the entire portion now extant, and it therefore embraces the whole of the fragment, not merely 96.6%. The percentages have been calculated on a slide-rule which gives an average accuracy of three digits.

Since the metre is all of one kind, the heavy rimed tetrameter, no significance can be attached to its use. That it is of this one kind is the crux of the matter, and that the variation which occurs in it is similarly noteworthy. If it would show anything, it would illustrate the truth that this is the most natural metre in which those who versified liked to write, and that its very naturalness is what has betrayed the playwright into by-ways like those of his successors.

II. Fulgens and Lucres[1]

Text: F. S. Boas and A. W. Reed, ed. (Oxford, 1926).
Date: 1497.[2]
Rhythm: light.
Prevailing metre: tetrameter rime royal.

Lines:	2353	%
Dissyllabic rime:	25	1.1
Redundant rime:	26	1.2
Rime lacking:	18	.8
Tetrameter rime royal:	1062	45.1
Tetrameter sixain coué:	988	42.4
Tetrameter octave couée:	88	3.7
Tetrameter ballad-six:	24	1.0
Tetrameter cinquain:[3]	20	.9
Miscellaneous:[4]	171	7.3

The first interlude, by the Rev. Henry Medwall, already shows form well in hand. The playwright is acutely conscious of his versification, but the versification itself is not academic, certainly not in accord with the Semitic and mediæval Latin attention to the individual syllable.[5] The result is that all kinds of unstressed syllables meet in a loquacious whole. The relative amount of variation in rime is not changed, but a new stanza form has appeared, most likely nothing more than a repeated redundancy. The comparatively large size of the miscellaneous schemes of rime, orderless as they are, indicates that the author was without great

[1] Text, pp. xxv-xxvi.

[2] Text, p. xx.

[3] Riming ababb; see Schipper, ii. 572-5.

[4] This includes various unreasoned forms like abbba (I. 479-483), aaxxbbbcc (I. 1250-1258), and the fragmentary interpolations like the cdd attached to the rime royal stanzas in series (II. 441-450), etc. The figures of textual reference will be those of lines unless it is otherwise specified.

[5] E. H. Sturtevant, "Commodian and Mediæval Rhythmic Verse," *Language* (1926), ii. 223-37.

care in the construction of his verses. He was content with the vague outlines of rime couée, and there he rested. Alliteration he eschewed, bending his attention to rime, and the riming is good;[6] his main interest lay elsewhere.

The two stanzaic systems are used with fine discrimination. For the more dignified scenes, those concerning Lucres and her father Fulgens,[7] and those of studied declamation by her suitors Cornelius and Flaminius,[8] the author has the light rime royal. This is used in careful contrast to the scenes of the sub-plot, which mimics the main theme not only in action but in its tailed verse.[9] Rime doggerel, or "rhythme peale meale,"[10] is the metre of the nameless boys and the Ancilla, like their conduct lacking in dignity. The verse is continually varying between these two forms, the playwright balancing one against the other with remarkable precision.

The result of perusing this first interlude is to be convinced of the utter consciousness with which Medwall wrought his verse, to feel that he was endeavoring perfectly to adapt the metre to the situation. It was not a particularly artistic adaptation—and the reasons are apparent—but it did serve to show that there was method in the use of the two schemes. Whether or not he was aware that he was setting a precedent in the tradition of this new drama cannot be known, but the precedent was set; and it was long before the advent of the easily manipulated racking tetrameter, the paced blank verse, and the merest of prose—sometimes tagged, sometimes not—came to create a ready and easy way for the manufacture of interludes.

[6] "Bargyn/playne" (II. 130/3) is the exception rather than the rule.

[7] I. 410-476.

[8] II. 356-389 concerns the suit of Cornelius; B finishes up the rime royal (387-389), which is later resumed (II. 404-807). B, however, assists once again with the measure (II. 768-781) although occasionally interrupted by Lucres. The 400 lines are of impure rime royal and include a ballad-six (II. 700-705, with which Flaminius concludes his harangue) and a doubled measure riming ababb bcbcc (II. 720-730); it has no significance.

[9] I. 354-393, 779-985, etc.

[10] The term given it by Richard Stanyhurst in the preface to his translation of Vergil; see p. 12, n. 47.

III. Nature[1]

Text: Brandl, pp. 73-158.
Date: 1500.[2]
Rhythm: light.
Prevailing metre: pentameter rime royal.

Lines:	2861	%
Dissyllabic rime:	47	1.7
Redundant rime:	5	.2
Latin rime:	1	—
Rime lacking:	10	.4
Unrimed Latin:	1	—
Linkage:	11	.4
Prose:	5	.2
Pentameter rime royal:	1099	38.5
Sixain coué:	759	26.6
Octave couée:	521	18.2
Tetrameter rime royal:	175	6.1
Dix-huitain coué:[3]	54	1.8
Tetrameter couplets:	16	.6
Pentameter couplets:	14	.5
Pentameter ballad-eight:	8	.3
Miscellaneous:[4]	207	5.9

Henry Medwall's other surviving interlude is built along lines similar to those of *Fulgens and Lucres.* Nature with a long speech in rime royal[5] opens the play, and in this measure discourses at length to Man, Sensuality, and Reason who likewise makes reply. The verse keeps up through the dignified *débat* until Man has decided, on the advice of Mundus,

[1] Text, pp. xxxvii-xxxviii; Bond, p. lxxxiv; Ramsay, pp. cxl-cxli.

[2] Text, p. xliv.

[3] In tetrameter riming abbbacccdeeedfeeef. Another e-rime is wheeled into the burden of the next group before the bob, f (I. 638-674).

[4] The same sort of thing (I. 836-950) that is to be found in *Fulgens and Lucres*, p. 16, n. 4. There are straggling triplets plus a half-line (II. 326-329), various illegitimate rimings like abacbddc ddde fffc (II. 400-412), and variations on the theme of rime royal.

[5] I. 1-106. The rime royal continues.

to put Innocency behind him as the verse falls into a species of tail-rime.[3] Worldly Affection and the vices plead their case before Man, in rime royal again,[6] and in rime couée overpower his scruples.[7] The two sentences of prose are spoken by Pride into Sensuality's ear *sonorâ voce*,[8] a method of presentation better adapted to such a device than that of including it in the tail-rime scheme.[9] Man goes off with Sensuality and the forces of evil remain; Worldly Affection and Pride talk over old times in the tavern in erratic rime couée[10] (in which rime royal irregularly irrupts) to relate an anecdote or to press the point that is being made.[11] Reason enters as Worldly Affection departs, and the "decay" of Man is lamented in rime royal[12] and tail-rime.[13] Man and rime royal come on together,[14] but the verse drops off to rime couée until "Shamfastnes" goes out, when Man and Reason converse in the Chaucerian measure.[15]

Reason and Man begin the second part with a long dialogue in rime royal.[16] The verse, in the second temptation scene and the natural upshot of Man's weakness, becomes a mixture of tail-rime and couplets,[17] with two stanzas of rime royal to lend weight to the remarks of Pride.[18] The matter of the morality having been got through in careless rime couée, Reason weans Man from his pleasure and brings him

[6] I. 675-723.

[7] I. 724-1051.

[8] Text, p. 99, after I. 836.

[9] J. F. Macdonald, "The Use of Prose in English Drama before Shakespeare," *University of Toronto Quarterly* (1933), ii. 465-81.

M. Muncaster, "The Use of Prose in Elizabethan Drama," *Modern Language Review* (1919), xiv. 10-5.

[10] I. 1052-1292.

[11] I. 1052-1058, 1113-1140, 1145-1158, 1163-1169, 1273-1279.

[12] I. 1293-1306.

[13] I. 1307-1320.

[14] I. 1321-1327.

[15] I. 1391-1397.

[16] II. 1-80.

[17] II. 81-1012.

[18] II. 304-317.

back to repent in a long scene of rime royal that terminates the play.[19]

The invitation to compare this interlude with *Fulgens and Lucres* is strong enough to point out the presence of less prosodic coherence in this play. The rime royal is used to begin both halves and to lend gravity to the pronouncements of Reason and Nature, as well as to terminate the work with the restoration of Man to virtue. Thus the outlines of Medwall's dramatic purpose are sufficiently clear, but there is not the hard and fast delineation that would keep Pride to rime couée. On the whole, it is the same system as that of the earlier and more artistic interlude, but the peripheral lines are more blurred. For the lighter scenes in which the vices disport themselves, rime couée is the vehicle; and for the earnest scenes of induction, virtuous persuasion, and ultimate triumph of good through penitence, the more sedate rime royal is employed. It is easily seen that in this interlude too Henry Medwall was thoroughly aware of his two contrasting rime schemes, and that (except for the careless element that manufactured curious combinations) he allowed his talent so to be parted yet bound.

[19] II. 1013-1422. It is not all in strict rime royal: e.g. ababbabbcc (1076-1085), and the true ballad-eight (1344-1351).

IV. The Droichis [Dwarf's] Part of the Play[1]

Text: J. Small, ed., *The Poems of William Dunbar* (Edinburgh, 1893. 3 vols.), ii. 314-320.
Date: 1503.[2]
Prevailing metre: light octave couée.

Lines:	176	%
Dissyllabic rime:	7	4.0
Light octave couée:	126	71.6
Heavy octave couée:	50	28.4

To William Dunbar is often ascribed this "littil interlud," which is written exclusively in rime couée of octave stanzas.[3] The first six of these stanzas are shorter in the verses than the rest, and a heavy iambic tread is imparted at the entrance of the "fule," but he soon goes off into lighter tetrameters when he begins to speak of his own ancestry and Finn MacCumhaill. There seems to be little reason for the leaven that has come into his "pairt," and one merely notes the change. The iambics also mark the entrance of blind Harry Hubbilshow, who settles into his dramatic monologue in the lighter measure.

[1] K. Luick, "Zur Metrik der mittelenglischen reimend-alliterierenden Dichtung," *Anglia* (1889), xii. 443.
[2] Eckhardt, i. 41.
[3] Four stresses in the wheel, two in the bob.

V. The World and the Child (Mundus et Infans)[1]

Text: Manly, i. 353-385.
Date: 1509.[2]
Rhythm: light.
Alliteration: predominant.
Prevailing metre: tetrameter octave couée.

Lines:	973	%
Dissyllabic rime:	19	2.0
Identical rime:	4	.4
Rime lacking:	12	1.2
Tetrameter octave couée:	520	53.5
Tetrameter quatrain:	92	9.5
Treizain:[3]	78	8.0
Trimeter octave couée:	48	4.9
Douzain coué:[4]	24	2.5
Neuvain:[5]	18	1.9
Seizain coué:[6]	16	1.6
Dimeter sixain coué:	12	1.2
Ballad-six:	6	.6
Cinquain:[7]	5	.5
Common measure:	4	.4
Pentameter quatrain:	4	.4
Miscellaneous:[8]	50	5.1

[1] H. N. MacCracken, "A Source of Mundus et Infans," *Publications of the Modern Language Association* (1908), xxiii. 487; Ramsay, pp. cxliii-cxliv; Reyher, p. 51; Saintsbury, i. 341; Schipper, i. 238-41.

[2] Eckhardt, i. 17.

[3] Thirteen lines of four stresses, made of two quatrains and a coda (the cinquain, n. 7) in the rhythm of common measure but riming cdddc: 131-143, 212-266, 274-287, 478-490, 546-558; this last group is a different kind of treizain arising from an octave couée plus the five-line coda.

[4] An octave couée to which another four lines, dddb, have been added (308-319, 850-861).

[5] In this interlude the stanza of nine lines consists of a tetrameter quatrain followed by the cinquain-coda.

[6] The alternation of rime in the tail holds this structure together: aaab cccd eeeb fffd (559-582).

[7] The five-line coda standing alone (648-652). Its rimes are abbba, its stresses 34443.

[8] Airy combinations for which the alliterative character of the verse is responsible, like the tetrametric abccbaccc (757-766), echo of the compound measures above. Rime is abstained from in certain quatrains (623-626, 783-786).

Manifold and crude are the verse forms of this early play. The syllabication is exceedingly erratic, which lends to the verse a buoyance not unfitting; the rimes are good. A case for five bob-wheel stanzas has been made out,[9] an atavism not elsewhere apparent in the interludes: the whole drama is a farrago of alliterative verse to which bringing order is difficult. To relate the different kinds of versifying to action, character, or anything else is out of the question. One merely notes the type of stanza and passes on. The author appears to have had no motive in mind when he selected his schemes for this work but constructed his elaborate stanzas as the whim beguiled him.

Mundus begins in alliterative tumbling measure with alternate rime,[10] and Infans follows.[11] With the appearance of Infans as Wanton, as he proclaims himself to be, the verse changes to rime couée *en huit*.[12] Having begun the interlude with self-exegesis, the pair is superseded by Lust and Liking, who speaks for one stanza in the treizain,[13] the rime couée then returning in its pristine form. Manhood rambles on in a hemistichic sixain coué,[14] but the staple of verse is soon returned. Manhood and Mundus use the treizain twice;[15] the metre reverts to rime couée, and another bob-wheel strophe is devoted to a dialogue between Manhood and Conscience.[16] The octave couée, almost unbroken,[17] runs on to the light quatrains of Conscience[18] and the heavier quatrains of Perseverance.[19] The bob-wheel measure with its five-

[9] Ramsay, p. cxliv. It is the treizain of n. 3 above.

[10] 1-24.

[11] 25-51.

[12] 52-130. At first the *frons* has four beats and the *cauda* three.

[13] 131-143.

[14] 184-187. The *frons* is printed in one line, the *cauda* in the next.

[15] 212-266, 275-287.

[16] 478-490.

[17] Manhood cuts it down to three beats (499-518) and adds three riming Skeltonics (519-521). His song (700-705) and the cinquain intervene.

[18] 721-736.

[19] 745-756.

line coda comes in sporadically for Manhood[20] and for Folly,[21] but it bears no significance. Conscience concludes a long screed with this coda or cinquain as if to presage the coming of Manhood (with whom it does seem casually to be identified), now grown old and decrepit.[22] The hapless hero now uses the tumbling quatrains to begin his address to all who will listen,[23] and it passes through the octave couée[24] and Skeltonic triplets[25] to come wearily to rest in the coda *in cinque.*[26] His breath is short, and he speaks in the tailed doggerel of two or three beats.[27] Perseverance briefly restores the tetrameter octave couée[28] that fulfills the prosodic destiny of the interlude, whatever it is. Perseverance finishes with a prayer in ballad-six of four stresses.[29]

The noteworthy elements of the prosody in *The World and the Child* are the preponderance of alliteration, the unique cinquain-coda, the lack of couplets, the revival of the bob-wheel stanza, the foundation of octave couée on which the last is based, and finally the lack of well defined significance in the use of the various metres. The hero of the interlude, Manhood (previously Infans, later Age), is sometimes favored with the unique cinquain, and to a certain extent it distinguishes him from the rest. Conscience admonishes in light alternate rime; Perseverance's is heavy. To discover more than this is to discover more than the unknown author infused: his liberties with the many schemes he nonchalantly uses are evidence that he had little method in the making of his verse, and still less in its more cerebral and dramatic aspect.

[20] 549-553, 635-639.
[21] 635-639, 648-652.
[22] 745-766. The last five lines are the cinquain-coda.
[23] 767-782.
[24] 783-790.
[25] 791-796.
[26] 797-810.
[27] 827-832, 841-861. With 850 the tailed rime becomes trimeter.
[28] 862-973.
[29] 974-979.

VI. Wealth and Health[1]

Text: F. Holthausen, ed. (Heidelberg, 1922).
Date: 1510.[2]
Rhythm: light.
Prevailing metre: tetrameter octave couée.

Lines:	951	%
Dissyllabic rime:	37	3.9
Identical rime:	4	.4
Redundant rime:	1	.1
Rime lacking:	17	1.8
Tetrameter octave couée:	625	65.7
Pentameter rime royal:	126	13.3
Tetrameter couplets:	93	9.8
Pentameter couplets:	44	4.6
Pentameter quatrain:	8	.8
Pentameter ballad-six:	6	.6
Miscellaneous:[3]	49	5.2

The "Enterlude of Welth and Helth" is for the most part a study in the octave couée.[4] It varies by the omission of a semi-stanza at times[5] and at other times of lines, sometimes achieving strange rimes[6] and extra hemistrophes.[7] When the ballad measure of six lines occurs, it is by the accident of dropping the fifth line from the rime royal.[8] The other schemes come and go, but the burden of the interlude which Wit, Wealth, Liberty, and Will bear is of the rime couée.

The play is more than half done by the time the heavy rime royal makes its appearance with Remedy,[9] who comes

[1] Text, pp. x-xiv.

[2] Text, pp. xvii-xviii.

[3] Including couplets added to the stanzas of rime royal (596-606, 556-571). The scheme is that of rime royal; but see below, n. 8.

[4] The wheeling lines have four stresses, those in the bob three.

[5] 44, 92, 168, etc.

[6] Mary/tary/Libertie (330/1/2).

[7] 657, 702, etc.

[8] 590-595; see p. 122, n. 6.

[9] 528-534.

to restore the wayward protagonists, erring in the defiles of the octave couée, to the paths of virtue. Wealth baulks at the reformation, and he answers in the couplets[10] to which he had been introduced (among other things) by Hans Beerpot, the "drunken Fleming."[11] Remedy pursues Wealth in rime royal,[12] the interruption in couplets of Health and his friends notwithstanding.[13] Not until Will and Wit return do the octaves couées come back.[14] Thereafter verse and action go merrily on in the doggerel vein until Remedy returns with rime royal, but it is short-lived.[15] Hans reappears in character as the verse moves in the light fours, Remedy not objecting.[16] Before returning to the vicious tail-rime, a passage in pentameter quatrains slips in: Health is ill and his conscience hurts.[17]

Wit and Will reënter to the accompaniment of rime couée in all gaiety[18] and have the courage even to mimic Remedy in his own rime royal.[19] A brief round of conversation in couplets[20] is followed by the exhortation to righteousness of Remedy and the repentance of all the "ryotoures" in rime royal for a stately close.[21] The lines with which the play ends, a prayer for Queen Elizabeth, seem to have been added a half-century later and are quite unlike (sc. in scheme) any others to be found in this interlude: Remedy, who speaks, has at last relinquished his rime royal.

In presenting the metrical procession of this play, the interest of the writer in the form of his work becomes apparent. Until the middle of the play is reached, he does not seem to become awake to variety but remains faithful to the waist-

[10] 535-536.
[11] 386-424.
[12] 537-543, 556-569, 572-585, 596-602.
[13] 544, 554-555, etc.
[14] 607-726.
[15] 729-735.
[16] 740-770.
[17] 771-805.
[18] 809-828.
[19] 858-864.
[20] 865-882.
[21] 883-945.

and-tail measure. Hans explodes the scheme with a travesty of rime royal that is best alluded to as couplets,[22] but the metre soon returns to its old ways. The entrance of the healing power, Remedy, is underscored by the Chaucerian stave that Medwall had consecrated a decade before. Metre from this point forward is varied to suit the nature of the situation. Following the lead of the chaplain at Ely, the lighter episodes are written in the doggerel rime and the weightier ones in the rime royal. Both types are punctuated for the sake of variety, it is likely, by couplets in the early approach to active conversation. What stands out in this case as in the first of the interludes is the continual balancing of the system of rime couée with that of rime royal accordingly as the passage is of a light or serious character.

[22] 386-392.

VII. (The Nature of) the Four Elements[1]

Text: J. T. Fischer, ed., *Marburger Studien zur englischen Philologie* (1903), v.
Date: 1512.[2]
Rhythm: light.
Prevailing metre: sixain coué.

Lines:[3]	1433	%
Dissyllabic rime:	36	2.5
Redundant rime:	58	4.1
Rime lacking:	39	2.7
Linkage:	4	.3
Sixain coué:	798	55.7
Pentameter rime royal:	354	24.7
Pentameter ballad-eight:	40	2.8
Octave couée:	40	2.8
Neuvain coué:[4]	36	2.5
Tetrameter couplets:	25	1.7
Dimeter couplets:	8	.6
Common measure:	4	.3
Miscellaneous:[5]	128	7.9

The metrical aspect of *The Four Elements* suggests, like the title, a direct reversion to *Nature*. The exhilarating John Rastell used the three main systems of our prosody: couplets, ballad-measures, and tail-rime. To speak generally, the ballad-measures are heavy in line, while the couplets and rimes couées are light.

The heavy pentameter rime royal opens the drama as the Messenger and the leading characters expound their natural

[1] Text, pp. 27-37; Brandl, pp. xxxvii-xxxviii; Ramsay, pp. cxli-cxlii; Saintsbury, i. 339-40; Schipper, i. 291.

[2] Eckhardt, i. 19.

[3] Exclusive of song; see p. 7, n. 24.

[4] A sixain coué longer by half.

[5] With various combinations like aababccx (413-420), aabccxc (922-928), aabbbcccddcee (1005-1018), and the thirteen assorted lines 1397-1409.

history without let or hindrance[6] until the vices appear.[7] Sensual Appetite, agonist perhaps, starts off in what is most easily called rimed tetrameter,[8] which rapidly dwindles to Skeltonics,[9] and then settles into a doggerel coué that omits rime unrestrainedly.[10] There are a few interruptions in this scheme,[11] but they amount to nothing, and the vicious rime couée rolls merrily on. It is of a sixain pattern; but when Ignorance appears, it changes to the strophe of eight lines.[12] Couplets irrupt when the dancers sing without as prelude to their entertainment,[13] but the sixain coué returns to conclude the play.

The conclusion one comes to is that Rastell began his geographical play fully intending to reserve the heavy dignified ballad-measure (even with a sort of internal discrimination) for the scenes of uplifting influence, and the light rime doggerel for the scenes of merriment. Thus the beginning; but when it became time to revert to the heavy rime royal with the entrance of Experience and Studious Desire,[14] the swing of the doggerel could not be halted, and the men of virtue speak with the same prosodic vulgarity as the men of vice. Schematic division of scene is discarded, and Rastell, his metrical purpose having fallen by the way, finishes in a swirl of rime couée with no regard for metrical differentiation.

[6] 1-404.

[7] Without any indication of entrance in 405. Nature, however, departs from the ballad stave of seven lines (rime royal) to that of eight (Monk's Tale stanza) by the insertion of a b-line after the sixth. It appears in the longest speech (274-288) and twice reappears (317-332, 383-390).

[8] 405-411.

[9] 413-419.

[10] 421-1319.

[11] 592-602, 884-891, 1005-1017.

[12] 1144-1151.

[13] 1320-1325.

[14] Before 664. Similar passages in which one might be led to expect the ballad-eights and -sevens are 1038-1141, 1434-1457.

VIII. Hickscorner[1]

Text: Manly, i. 386-420.
Date: 1512.[2]
Rhythm: light.
Prevailing metre: tetrameter couplets.

Lines:	1026	%
Dissyllabic rime:	43	4.2
Identical rime:	2	.2
Redundant rime:	28	2.7
Rime lacking:	16	1.6
Tetrameter couplets:	377	36.7
Tetrameter sixain coué:	102	10.0
Tetrameter neuvain coué:	72	7.0
Tetrameter octave couée:	64	6.2
Tetrameter rime royal:	63	6.1
Tetrameter ballad-six:	60	5.8
Tetrameter quatrain:	44	4.3
Tetrameter ballad-eight:	32	3.1
Dimeter couplets:	23	2.2
Trimeter couplets:	6	.6
Trimeter quatrain:	4	.4
Miscellaneous:[3]	179	17.5

This interlude is also a chaos of verse. Forms change for no reason from rime royal to couplets to rime couée as they please, nor have the linear irregularities the condoning grace of alliteration. The preponderance of the dramatic doggerel, i.e. light tetrameter couplets, shows that the interlude had reached prosodic maturity, that it was not the inchoate welter, for instance, of *Youth, Liberality and Prodigality,* or indeed *The World and the Child* in this same tradition. Comparison with this last-named interlude is favored by similarity of theme, but in a few years great verse-change had been

[1] Ramsay, p. cxliii; Reyher, p. 52; Saintsbury, i. 341.

[2] Whiting, p. 83.

[3] Schemes like abbcc in trimeter (151-155) among rimes couées, and the tetrameters riming abcaddefgg (260-269) and aaaxaabbcccdd (304-316) are here included among others. There is also a noteworthy example of a refrain's occurring in a douzain coué (549-560). It rimes aaaB cccB dddB; the lines of the burden have four beats, and the refrain has three.

wrought. Double rimes were themselves doubled in quantity, while those omitted remained at par. Alliteration had gone and in its stead came rime: were one looking for a reliable illustration of electromotive replacement in prosody, these interludes would serve.[4] Rime couée is fading, alternate rime increasing, and couplets have already begun to bear sway. In dramatic prosody as in language, development corresponds with simplification if not improvement.

To review the metres in the order of their appearance is fruitless. Pity and Contemplation speak in alternate rime[5] that occasionally is modulated into the Monk's Tale stanza[6] and the rime royal,[7] which is congenial to Perseverance.[8] Freewill and Imagination use rime couée,[9] but they are by no means confined to it.[10] Alternate rime comes and goes, sometimes tagged with rime, which makes it look like a ballad-six.[11] The ballad measures themselves seem to be concentrated more toward the beginning[12] and the third quarter of the play;[13] rime couée darts in and out. Bad verse[14] is,

[4] If alliteration is considered as head-rime, the anatomy of versification points to the more recent caudal location of the consonance. The delaying of the similar sound until the end of line lends a dramatic effect of its own, one which must necessarily be absent in alliterative lines, where the object is to have done with the parallel sounds as quickly as convenient.

[5] 1-16, 40-55.

[6] 25-31, 63-70.

[7] 33-39.

[8] 75-81, 86-92. The difficulty attending the construction of this type of verse suggests an author's wry smile on giving this strophe to Perseverance.

[9] 156-230.

[10] Tetrameter quatrains are used mostly by Freewill (420-427, 511-518), and by Imagination (270-273, 402-405, 487-490; the rimes in 420-423 and 487-490 are distributed abba). Freewill wanders even into rime royal (727-733).

[11] 709-714, 721-726, 630-635. Speculation ends only in doubt.

[12] 1-118.

[13] 630-888.

[14] The stresses in the neuvain coué, 620-629 (622 is a redundancy), run 4443434322. The dramatic doggerel rimes keep step, 473-484: quarrel/steal (475/6), bag/sad (477/8), gyves/heels (479/80); hose-rings/bonds (516/7).

on the whole, complemented by bad use of it; it is not credible that the dramatist gave its form any thought whatever but rimed just as the words came to him.

As the bob-wheel stanza was unique in *The World and the Child,* so there is a strange group of lines given to Pity in the middle of *Hickscorner.*[15] It appears to be a song in tail-rime, but there is no indication of this in Wynkyn de Worde's printing. The form with its refrain is so strange, however, that it suggests a specimen of mediæval poetic activity,[16] of iambic tetrameter *trimembris* with a three-iambic *differentia* repeated.[17] The rimes are good, and the treatment of the feet is appropriate to the subject. As for a dirge, the lines are very heavy at the outset, and then extra syllables steal in to lighten the verse. A bit of light tetrameter octave couée[18] is followed by a similar stave with a refrain also;[19] with the end of this refrain the verse changes abruptly to tetrameter couplets.[20] From a discussion of the dramatic prosody this song (for so it deserves to be considered) is best omitted,[21] and however one looks at it, it is clearly not a factor to alter the opinion already advanced: that the author of *Hickscorner,* even more than he of *The World and the Child,* ignored the prosodic significance of what he was writing but used the familiar patterns as they came to hand without thought of relating them to what was happening in the drama.

[15] 549-600.

[16] See Berdan, pp. 125-6, 149-53.

[17] Anapæsts slip in among the iambs to alleviate the dolor of the verse. The beginning is certainly heavy, the first line actually spondaic (549).

[18] 561-592. In this prosier part the rimes go rapidly down-hill: wages/haunts/gyves (585/6/7).

[19] 593-600.

[20] 601-619. When Pity speaks after his release, the lines become anomalously heavy (611-619).

[21] Although not omitted from the tabulated summary.

IX. (The Interlude of) Youth[1]

Text: W. Bang and R. B. McKerrow, ed., *Materialen zur Kunde des älteren englischen Dramas* (1905), xii. 1-24.
Date: 1512.[2]
Rhythm: light.
Prevailing metre: tetrameter couplets.

Lines:[3]	786	%
Dissyllabic rime:	14	1.8
Identical rime:	4	.5
Redundant rime:	10	1.3
Rime lacking:[4]	107	13.6
Tetrameter couplets:	593	90.5
Tetrameter quatrain:[5]	32	4.0
Tetrameter sixain coué:	24	3.0
Leash:	20	2.5

The brief "Enterlude of Youth" contains but two kinds of metre: rime couée *en six*, and tumbling verse that sometimes rimes in alternation. Versification is extremely poor, there being no syllabic method worth noting, words are repeated frequently for the sake of rime, and an average of one line in eight is unrimed.[6] Rime couée appears sparingly without purpose in the words of Youth,[7] Riot,[8] and Pride[9] in scenes during which temptation occurs; but encouragement in the path of dalliance is by no means confined to the few interpolations. One might, in fact, consider them as mere accidents in the compounding of wretched verse.

[1] Brandl, p. lxi; Saintsbury, i. 341.

[2] Text, p. xiv.

[3] From the edition of John Waley, about 1557. The Copland edition (text, pp. 25-48) of about three years later adds a riming line after 784.

[4] There are also two Latin rimes, one of which appears in abbreviation: man/iusticiã (523/4).

[5] Half the time riming abab, otherwise abba.

[6] The following, on the other hand, are rimes: mind/thing (104/5), men/them/amend (765/6/7).

[7] 291-294.

[8] 447-452.

[9] 650-655.

The orthodox abab-rimes are for the most part collected in the scene[10] wherein Youth vaunts himself before Humility, who opposes him: "Wherefore your brains we will steer and keel[11] you a little again." The fever abates in the tumbling verse that makes up the body of the play. The heterodox abba-rimes seem, like the tail-rime, to be due more to chance than intent and have no connexion with anything.[12] The only fit observation one can make on the prosody of *Youth* is that it is congruous in its badness and futility.

[10] 439-452.

[11] Greasy Joan's work at the end of *Love's Labours Lost.*

[12] 39-42, 354-357, 552-555.

X. Magnificence[1]

Text: Ramsay, pp. 1-80.
Date: 1515.[2]
Rhythm: light.
Alliteration: remarkably pronounced.
Prevailing metre: tetrameter couplets.

Lines:	2553	%
Dissyllabic rime:	254	10.0
Trisyllabic rime:	4	.2
Identical rime:	6	.3
Redundant rime:	5	.2
Rime lacking:	13	.5
Tetrameter couplets:	1674	65.7
Tetrameter rime royal:	660	25.9
Dimeter rime royal:	77	3.0
Pentameter rime royal:	58	2.3
Tetrameter leash:	37	1.4
Dimeter couplets:	27	1.1
Dimeter leash:	15	.6
Pentameter couplets:	8	.3
Dimeter quatrain:	4	.2
Miscellaneous:[3]	7	.3

The two pillars upon which *Magnificence* rests are couplets and rime royal. The lines vary from two beats to six as occasion suits John Skelton, who has worked out a rime royal stanza in dimeter[4] bestowed upon a vice *solus,* Courtly Abusion. The Skeltonics and the leashes come and go because the author wills it. In the third scene, for example, Measure attempts to mediate between Liberty and Felicity on

[1] Text, pp. li-lxxi; one cannot presume to improve upon this elaborate study. See also Bond, p. lxxxiv; Reyher, pp. 55-9; Saintsbury, i. 335-7; Schipper, i. 233-42; Schröer, pp. 257-64.

[2] Text, p. xxii.

[3] Including French and Latin rimes and two curiously macaronic hexameters with internal rime at the penthemimeral cæsura (1155-1156).

[4] 835-911, a great *tour de force* inveighing against fashion. The French monometer sonnets of the nineteenth century are called to mind, e.g. the *Epitaphe d'une jeune fille* by Jules de Rességuier.

a matter philosophical, whether felicity can exist without freedom. The poet, apparently with his tongue in his cheek, presents the beginning of the arbitration not only in flagrant dimeter couplets but in the cruder leash;[5] but when Measure really begins his explanation, he uses the light tetrameter rime royal.[6] Leash serves the soliloquy of Counterfeit Countenance[7] to speak humorously of his various and excellent social standing, a theme congenial to the author of *The Bowge of Court.* Fancy, who is quite mad, enters with his hawk and apostrophizes him (calling him "owl") in Skeltonic leash.[8] His admiration for the bird is interrupted by clowning with the audience. Folly later tags his tetrameters with nonsensical rimes to lash them together;[9] nearly the whole of scene 28 is made of reiterated rime.[10]

The more orthodox rime royal contains either four or five stresses. The pentameter is ten times as rare as the shorter form and is consecrated to the hero. Proud and fearless, he talks to himself,[11] unaware of the fate in store for him. Then, when Adversity has come to him replete with plagues and diseases, he laments his fate in two stanzas, the first of tetrameter rime royal[12] and the second of pentameter.[13] When Liberty in the following scene has sufficiently lectured him in tetrameter couplets, Magnificence is left all alone to beweep his outcast state in a stanza of heavy pentameter rime royal.[14] The same thing recurs later as before: a single sad strophe is the sum of scene 38.[15] Despair thereupon enters

[5] 87-113.

[6] 114-162.

[7] 410-493.

[8] 972-1007.

[9] 1804-1811.

[10] Except for the final couplet, the entire scene of 40 lines is wrought on five rimes. Magnificence tries in vain to dam the current of his insanity (1803-1842).

[11] Scene 27, 1797-1803.

[12] 2048-2054. These might just as well be taken as two specimens of light tetrameter rime royal. If the second be considered pentameter, its nature is heavy or iambic.

[13] 2055-2061.

[14] Scene 34, 2153-2159.

[15] 2277-2283.

with a recommendation to suicide and employs this heavy measure for rehearsing Magnificence's divers sins.[16] The repentance of the erring and edified Magnificence having been achieved, Sad Circumspection comes upon Stage 5 in order to go over the whole history once again and to make solicitous inquiry into the reasons for the tragedy.[17] This is the last appearance of the five-beat rime royal. The lines are rather light and therefore of greater length than usual, but one staff of this is sufficient, and the verse becomes settled into the tetrameter.

The case of the rime royal in light fours most actively concerns the first two scenes. Felicity condenses the interlude by way of introduction into four stanzas of rime royal. Liberty enters, begins to argue with Felicity in tetrameter couplets,[18] and receives a formal reply in the Chaucerian measure of four beats. A brief passage of Skeltonics follows,[19] after which Liberty makes his position clear, and the second scene is concluded.[20] A long passage of rime royal supervenes in the third scene.[21] Measure, who interrupted the debate between Felicity and Liberty at the beginning of this scene with tetrameter couplets and Skeltonic leash, begins moulding his language in rime royal. He speaks with dignity, saying that he should have dominion over Wealth. After briefly demurring, the three characters on-stage decide that they belong together,[22] and Magnificence enters and joins them.[23] As the *camaraderie* and action go forward, save for a short interruption in couplets by Fancy,[24] Magnificence is permitted to remain and to speak like the others.[25] Tetrameter couplets then return with the advent of Counter-

[16] 2284-2306.
[17] 2419-2425.
[18] 29-40.
[19] 55-66.
[20] 67-80.
[21] 114-324.
[22] 128-162.
[23] 163.
[24] An extra line (252) makes the rime royal stave look like a quatrain and two couplets.
[25] To the end of scene 6, 251-324.

feit Countenance as the plot of the play is advanced.[26] Leash, noted above, reappears; after a time it is followed by the Skeltonics of Cloaked Collusion,[27] in which the rogues lay their plans. "Hic deambulat" Cloaked Collusion, then, who soliloquizes in the light rime royal of four stresses, reviewing all his villainous characteristics, of which the chief is hypocrisy.[28] Further progress of the speech is halted by the coming of Courtly Abusion with a *Lied ohne Worte,*[29] and the measure lapses[30] until Crafty Conveyance restores it for his monologue.[31] He keeps talking about himself and the good work he does in petty larceny; when he has ceased, the action is shifted to the third Stage, "Delusion," where Magnificence and his friends are carrying forward the drama.[32] Conversation is in this case only a splice in rime royal between the monologue of Crafty Conveyance and that of Magnificence.[33] The latter is at the height of his power; ancient history he rehearses in full career to find an example of ambition satisfied like his own. Seventeen great generals pass in review, one of them later to prove the subject of an interlude,[34] and all seventeen are put down as inferior. This stream of self-appreciation is diverted by the coming of couplets with Courtly Abusion;[35] and except for the cases already noted, the measure departs from the interlude.

Skeltonics, or rimed hemistichs, are used with restraint. Except for the specimens already mentioned and stray couplets,[36] they come in leash. Stichomythia once employs them, and they are used to cap the extended hemistichic rime

[26] 325-409.

[27] 588-592.

[28] Scene 11, 689-744.

[29] 745-747.

[30] The dimeter rime royal of Courtly Abusion and a mixture of couplets, two and four beats to the line (i.e. lines riming with half-lines), bridge this gap.

[31] Scene 19, 1327-1374.

[32] 1375.

[33] 1457-1514.

[34] *King Darius.* 1488; see pp. 127-9.

[35] Scene 24 and beyond, 1515-1796.

[36] 799-800.

royal of Courtly Abusion;[37] they otherwise belong to the first six hundred lines of the play. Liberty and Fellowship protest to each other in them,[38] and they are the vehicle of Cloaked Collusion and Crafty Conveyance when they put their heads together.[39] The rest of the drama bears up under the usual rimed tetrameter, light and thoroughly irregular.

The most striking feature of John Skelton's dramatic prosody is the disregard of all the Latin he learned.[40] He follows the English tradition alone in his tetrameter couplets and in his rime royal. His use of these measures is sharply defined: rime royal is used to give weight to soliloquy of whatever kind, the verse of the protagonist being even somewhat heavier than that of the others. Scenes of indignity and altercation find use for Skeltonic couplets, and the bulk of the drama rocks forward on the light rimed fours. An extra stress may slip in to bear down upon the moral aspect, as in the case of Good Hope,[41] but rime scheme is what serves the playwright's purpose. Quite unlike the original methods of prosodic treatment, the varying of verse in *Magnificence* is extrinsic. There is no connexion between character and verse or between theme and verse; the bad characters and the good characters are at home in the two kinds.[42] On the whole, the use of couplets and rime royal seems to be owing only to the dramatist's desire to talk to his audience with more or less concentrated zeal. It betrays a lack of interest in character as such, and even in morality as such, morality play though this is. The discrimination of Henry Medwall finds no resonance in the extant work of Skelton, his greatest successor hitherto.[43]

[37] 917-918.

[38] 55-66.

[39] 588-592.

[40] See p. 194.

[41] 2325-2328.

[42] Rime couée is absent from the interludes for the first time.

[43] The lost play of *Nigramansir* (Necromancer) is said by Thomas Warton (*History of English Poetry* [London, 1824. 3 vols.], iii. 185-7) to have been composed in "a variety of measures, with shreds of Latin and French . . . but the devil speaks in the octave stanza." There is no specimen of an octave stanza in *Magnificence*.

XI. John the Evangelist

Text: J. S. Farmer, ed., "*Lost*" *Tudor Plays* (London, 1907), pp. 351-368.
Date: 1520.[1]
Rhythm: light.
Alliteration: marked.
Prevailing metre: tetrameter couplets.

Lines:	529	%
Dissyllabic rime:	62	11.7
Trisyllabic rime:	2	.4
Redundant rime:	18	3.4
Identical rime:	5	.9
Latin rime:	10	1.9
Unrimed Latin:	5	.9
Rime lacking:	19	3.6
Tetrameter couplets:	176	33.2
Tetrameter ballad-eight:	104	19.7
Trimeter sixain coué:	42	7.9
Tetrameter quatrain:	32	5.1
Trimeter neuvain coué:	18	3.4
Common measure:	12	2.3
Tetrameter sixain coué:	12	2.3
Tetrameter leash:	9	1.7
Tetrameter rime royal:	7	1.3
Trimeter couplets:	6	1.1
Trimeter quatrain:	4	.8
Miscellaneous:[2]	111	12.1

So strong is the tendency to alliteration[3] in *John the Evangelist* that the lineaments of riming methods are obscured. The beats themselves are almost impossible to discover, and very often it is necessary to make wild conjectures as to where the author expected them to fall. There is no evenness of distribution, and each line ought, if possible, to

[1] W. W. Greg, ed., for the Malone Society (London, 1907), p. vi; see also below, p. 199, n. 18.

[2] The alliterative quality of the verse makes for irregularities like the three- and four-stressed lines 77-89, axaaxabbxbxccccdd.

[3] And its attending illiteracy.

be scanned separately. The text, moreover, is corrupt; emendations and suggestions for revision have been frequent, and the very name of one of the chief characters, Irisdision, is in doubt. Farmer's facsimile reprint[4] is of no assistance; from this inchoate mass it is difficult to glean even the few prosodic facts which come under observation.

The great amount of ballad-eights is noteworthy. John begins the play with them[5] and Eugenio continues.[6] Irisdision early in the play also finds them suitable,[7] but thereafter they disappear, not to return until the end is in sight. In the final sermon of John they are restored,[8] and the play concludes with them in a curiously linked stanza with the religious words of its protagonist.[9]

Owing to the absence from the middle portion of the play of this ballad measure, its hemistrophic counterpart (the quatrain) is made to serve for the words of John and Eugenio.[10] Idleness, one of the less reputable group, is given the privilege of alternate rime,[11] but his case is exceptional. The vices speak in tail-rime,[12] in which Irisdision and Eugenio are content to join them.[13] Couplets sustain the burden of the interlude according to their usual practice.

When one has painted this outline with a broad brush, the work is accomplished, and one is left with the same conclusion that has been applicable to most of the interludes considered; namely, that for scenes of good and virtue the ballad stave was used, that for the scenes of vice and evil rime couée was

[4] 1907 [n. p.].

[5] 1-24.

[6] 25-31.

[7] 61-76. The last seven lines of his speech are in rime royal, but its existence as a separate kind of verse form is accidental.

[8] 455-508.

[9] A tetrametric amalgam riming ababbcdcddede.

[10] 192-205, 445-454.

[11] 371-374.

[12] 133-142, 165-178, 210-233, 297-302, etc.

[13] 125-130, 266-271, 432-444. The details of these rimes couées are in themselves interesting. The words of Irisdision have a Gilbertian air, and those of Actio (210-233) are in a series whose *caudae* are all of one rime.

judged fitting, and that couplets of varying sizes were used to fill the pores of the piece. The method of this prosodic treatment is more reversive than prospective; the quantity of alliteration links it with the dark backward of poetry and drama, going hand in hand with the use of the octastich in place of the smoother rime royal. The author was certainly conscious of his prosody, but not sufficiently conscientious to make good verse with it. He let the swing and feeble attempts at the rime schemes with which he was familiar carry him and his story along through the brief span of his drama.

XII. The Pardoner and the Friar[1]

Text: F. J. Child, ed., *Four Old Plays* (Cambridge, 1848), pp. 89-128.
Date: 1521.[2]
Rhythm: light.
Prevailing metre: tetrameter couplets.

Lines:	640	%
Dissyllabic rime:	64	10.0
Trisyllabic rime:	2	.3
Redundant rime:	2	.3
Identical rime:	1	.2
Rime lacking:[3]	3	.5
Tetrameter couplets:	414	64.6
Tetrameter quatrain:	210	32.8
Dimeter sixain coué:	12	1.9
Short measure:	4	.6

In what is probably the earliest of John Heywood's interludes the prosody is unique. The staple of verse is the dramatic doggerel which later came to be the most legitimate medium for the interlude. In the rimed tetrameter the entire dialogue of the Pardoner and the Friar takes place except for two short interruptions of rime doggerel: one by the Friar before prayers are begun,[4] and the other before the sermon.[5] The use of the tetrameter from then on is unbroken, but the rimes are ingeniously distributed. When either of the speakers has anything of length to say, he delivers his words in couplets; whenever there is an attempt at dialogue in which alternate lines are given to the same character, the verse turns

[1] Reyher, p. 59; Saintsbury, i. 338. The general discussion by W. Swoboda (*John Heywood als Dramatiker. Wiener Beiträge zur deutschen und englischen Philologie* [1888], iii. 83-107) of Heywood's prosody as exemplified in his dramatic works is based on the work of Jakob Schipper, *Altenglische Metrik* (Bonn, 1881).

[2] Eckhardt, i. 43.

[3] There is also a line of unrimed Latin (189).

[4] 73-78.

[5] 183-188.

to quatrains.[6] The consequence of this alternation of rime is extraordinary: each of the characters speaks, as it were, in couplets, tagging his own previous rime as he was accustomed to do in spite of the interruptions of his fellows. The fact that this is a true *débat* is by this means more forcibly presented to the audience, for it cannot help feeling that both Pardoner and Friar are making their set speeches in couplets whether or not a line slides in edgewise. The perfect symmetry of this arrangement would enhance the artificiality of the procedure, and it is easy to understand why this form was not adopted later by Heywood or his followers. It is as if each of the persons spoke his part alone in unvarying couplets without regard for the other. In view of the animation of Heywood's succeeding work, the deathly aspect of this double monologue—his various efforts to redeem it notwithstanding—must be ascribed to the foreign models on which he drew.

[6] The stichomythic passages in light tetrameter quatrains are to be found in 190-253, 316-343, 364-407, 440-509, 527-530.

XIII. Witty and Witless

Text: F. S. Fairholt, ed., for the Percy Society (1846), xx.[1]
Date: 1521.[2]
Rhythm: light.
Alliteration: abundant.
Prevailing metre: tetrameter couplets.

Lines:	702	%
Dissyllabic rime:	104	14.8
Tetrameter couplets:	655	93.3
Tetrameter rime royal:	35	5.0
Dimeter couplets:[3]	12	1.7

"A Dialogue of Wit and Folly," as this sketch is sometimes called, really concerns three persons who debate the subject of wit and folly in the tetrameter couplets germane to John Heywood. At the beginning of the text John and James are arguing in the light familiar scheme. John deprecates the "wyttles wretche" in a series of Skeltonics,[3] but the intermezzo is short and couplets are restored, interrupted only by little interjections. Many of the lines are divided between two characters, especially John and Jerome.[4] This is a device employed by Heywood with a frequency not elsewhere to be parallelled. With five stanzas of rime royal the discussion is brought to its close, apparently by Jerome, in words of admonition to the listeners.[5]

The manipulation of the three schemes of versification is seen to be without purpose. The swing of the Skeltonics adds a certain interest to the attack on stupidity, but as the writer proceeds with his work he becomes more and more sober in tenor until he reaches the final staves of rime royal, in which the edge of the moral is whetted. The use of the various devices is elementary, and at the end Heywood is pleased to atone for his Skeltonical caprice with solemn Chaucerian metre.

[1] The original, which is thought to be in Heywood's hand, lacks the introduction.

[2] Eckhardt, i. 43.

[3] 32-43.

[4] In the linear references, however, each half is considered a separate line.

[5] 687-721.

XIV. (The Play Called) The Four P's[1]

Text: J. Q. Adams, ed., *Chief Pre-Shakespearean Dramas* (Cambridge, 1924), pp. 367-384.
Date: 1521.[2]
Rhythm: light.
Prevailing metre: tetrameter couplets.

Lines:	1236	%
Dissyllabic rime:	170	13.8
Trisyllabic rime:	6	.5
Rime lacking:	7	.6
Tetrameter couplets:	1194	96.7
Tetrameter quatrain:	28	2.3
Tetrameter rime royal:	14	1.1

The manipulation of verse in "The playe called the foure PP." gave Heywood little trouble. The metre of the lines is the customary light tetrameter, and it is the sole type to make its appearance, although certain lines can hardly be scanned as other than iambic decasyllables.[3] The verse itself is very good and contains an unusual amount of polysyllabic rime, the rarity of whose presence is illustrative of the difficulty incurred in its practice. One line in seven is thus adorned in *The Four P's*.

The Palmer begins by speaking in alternate rime to introduce himself,[4] but he soon lapses into the dramatic doggerel that continues through the rest of the play. When the conclusion has been reached, the Palmer speaks an epilogue of religious tone in two stanzas of light rime royal.[5]

What was intended for an introduction became no introduction at all, and the playwright saw that it would be just as fitting for him to become settled as soon as possible into the rhythm of the four-beat doggerel which would carry the

[1] Brandl, p. lxi; Reyher, p. 59; Saintsbury, i. 337-8; Schipper, i. 291.
[2] Text, p. 367.
[3] Not to go beyond the concluding stanzas, e.g. 1223, 1232.
[4] 1-28. He keeps talking, however, until the Pardoner breaks in, 64.
[5] 1223-1236.

play. The prosody is without variation until Heywood is ready to send his audience home with a hortatory posy in a dignified measure that is sharply contrasted with the doggerel couplets. There is no internal attention to the versification; John Heywood used change in order to round off the edges of his work like many another who followed him. If the earliest date acceptable, 1521, be the true one, the dramatist must be charged with having overturned all the prosodic principles on which the early interlude was founded, to have reduced all the vari-colored schemes of rime couée to his own crepuscular four-footer, and to have saved distinction in the verse merely for the head and tail of the play. In establishing this normalized, loose tetrameter as the proper vehicle for the interlude he did away with the older forms in such a way as to set a precedent which the authors of *Respublica, Jacob and Esau,* and others were not slow to follow, since it lightened the cerebral effort involved in the versification of the drama. Heywood's sovereign disregard of the various verse forms is at his time without parallel and of precocious significance in the ontogeny of the sixteenth-century drama. So unique indeed has been the prosody of his work and of those which followed in its wake that they make a group apart, and to him their authorship is most easily ascribed.

XV. Godly Queen Hester[1]

Text: W. W. Greg, ed., *Materialen zur Kunde des älteren englischen Dramas* (Louvain, 1904), v.
Date: 1525.[2]
Rhythm: mixed.
Prevailing metre: sixain coué.[3]

Lines:	1180	%
Dissyllabic rime:	127	10.8
Trisyllabic rime:	2	.2
Redundant rime:	6	.5
Identical rime:	2	.2
Rime lacking:	35	3.0
Sixain coué:[4]	332	28.1
Pentameter rime royal:	325	27.6
Tetrameter rime royal:	280	23.7
Tetrameter couplets:	68	5.8
Neuvain coué:	36	3.0
Pentameter couplets:	14	1.2
Dimeter ballad-eight:	8	.7
Miscellaneous:[5]	117	9.9

[1] Ramsay, pp. cxvi-cxviii.

[2] Eckhardt, i. 3.

[3] But if the stanzas of rime royal be assayed together, they will far (23%) overbalance those of sixain coué; see also p. 130, n. 3.

[4] The printers of the 1561 edition, William Pickering and Thomas Hacket, have so rearranged the lines that the sixain is usually telescoped into four verses. As a rule, the wheel is printed in one line and the bob in the one following. This manner of printing enables the short lines to absorb redundancies (487, 558, etc.) and to introduce all kinds of irregularities; the 332 lines ought probably to be expanded to 500. The prevailing number of stresses to which rime is applied is two. See also p. 159, n. 4.

[5] Including a few lines of leash and unstudied schemes like abaccddeefgfhii (162-176) and the lines between the heavy and light rimes royal (244-261) in which are to be found traces of rime royal and ballad-six. There are examples of dimeter quatrains printed in two lines (992-995) and of aberrations from rime royal, e.g. abaxbcc followed by ababbaa (922-970). There is also an instance of Latin rime (970) in this place.

As the text now stands, it is practically impossible to catalogue the irregularities. A complete rewriting would be necessary.

In sharp contrast to the good verse of the fragmentary *King Ahasuerus and Queen Hester*[6] there is the garbled metrics of *Godly Queen Hester*. Rimes are bad,[7] syllables wander in and out of lines that make no pretense of regularity,[8] and the state of the text hinders one from getting much good from a study of its prosody. The general lineaments alone are discernible; furred as they are, it is these which we shall be obliged to trace.

The Prologue and King Ahasuerus start the play in rime royal,[9] a metre which returns frequently to adorn the speeches of the king,[10] Gentlemen,[11] Mordecai,[12] Haman,[13] Esther,[14] Pursuivant,[15] divers Jews,[16] and Arbona.[17] The conclusion to which the reader is led is that this is the Skeltonic method of employment, that of underscoring important speeches by the chief persons of the drama whatever their position and moral tenets may be. This metre is also used by the king and queen to provide a sort of epilogue for the play.[18] Its one great consistency is that Hardy-Dardy the Vice is never permitted to use it. His field is tumbling verse and tail-rime, and in it he disports himself to the detriment of the verse itself.[19] Rime couée is the well-caparisoned vehicle for the scenes of vice, their peculiar property.[20] Pride begins and

[6] A much later production; see p. 220.

[7] Sured/honor (22/3), poet/feats (1027/9), brass/worse (1031/3).

[8] The versifying is generally worst in the vice-scenes, especially 437-451; 442 has seventeen syllables. See below, n. 19.

[9] 1-49, 54-84, 87-100, etc.

[10] 106-112, 132-138, 223-229, 262-268, 327-333, 758-769, 869-877, 922-970, 1073-1079.

[11] 22-86.

[12] 141-161, 171-183.

[13] 211-217, 588-608, 611-631, 695-757, 985-991.

[14] 273-293, 311-324, 853-868, 1082-1151.

[15] 188-208.

[16] 813-852.

[17] With Ahasuerus, 1003-1006; otherwise, 1057-1070.

[18] 1162-1175. The play runs on in couplets for five more lines.

[19] 636-691, 1010-1056.

[20] 338-580, 636-691, 791-812, 1010-1056.

the rest follow. It is rime couée of Skeltonics; one recalls that there had been no rime couée in *Magnificence*.[21]

The thought of variation in metrics was therefore well entrenched in the mind of the playwright. Rime royal was allotted for purposes of gravity to characters of consequence whatever their moral tropism,[22] rime couée was the province of the vices, and tumbling verse was used to fill in the hiatus, welding the various forms to one another in the effort to unify the production. The scheme is simple, sharp in concept, and carried throughout the drama. The author, extremely conscious of these three metrical estates, used them carefully and cautiously to the end that the audience should separate the main part of the drama from the comic scenes and to give respectful ear to his pronouncements. Notwithstanding his careless attitude toward the individual line,[23] the versification must be acknowledged workmanlike and conscientious.

[21] A comparison of general statistics from *Magnificence* and *Godly Queen Hester* does little to settle the question of John Skelton's authorship. There is a certain similarity in the distribution of rime-schemes, but the internal evidence weakens the theory:

	Couplets %	Rime Royal %	Polysyllabic rime %
Godly Queen Hester:	7.0	51.3	11.0
Magnificence:	67.4	28.2	10.2

Alone the quantity of polysyllabic rime remains proportionately equal. A counting of syllables would tend, it is reasonable to divine, to substantiate this thesis: that from the evidence provided by the prosody alone, *Godly Queen Hester* cannot with justice be ascribed to Skelton.

[22] It may be worth while to mention that the lighter tetrameter rime royal falls to the lot of the queen, while "Assuerus" speaks in the pentameter. To this there are slight exceptions (Esther: 273-279, 311-324; Ahasuerus: 106-112, 132-138, 262-268, 996-1002, 1073-1079), but the rule holds. Since Haman speaks in the rime royal of both four and five beats (four: 695-701, 709-715, 751-757; five: 702-708, 716-736, 744-750), it is doubtful that there existed any ulterior motive in lengthening and weighting the stanzas given to the king.

[23] Judging from a metrical point of view. Dramatically, of course, the aphæretic, syncopated, and apocopated lines of Hardy-Dardy are quite effective, like the liberties taken with the lines of tail-rime. The same cannot be said for the rime royal. The tale of Esther is notoriously the least godly of all the Biblical books, and the versification of this measure keeps it fair company.

XVI. Calisto and Melibea[1]

Text: W. W. Greg, ed., for the Malone Society (London, 1908).
Date: 1530.[2]
Rhythm: light.
Prevailing metre: tetrameter rime royal.

Lines:	1089	%
Dissyllabic rime:	84	7.7
Identical rime:	2	.2
Unrimed Latin:	1	.1
Linkage:	2	.2
Tetrameter rime royal:	1087	99.8
Tetrameter couplet:	2	.2

From the summary above it will be seen that practically all this drama is in the light rime royal, a phenomenon almost without parallel in the interludes.[3] Except for the two extraneously rimed lines given to Melibea,[4] the entire play is written in the seven-line ballad stanza. Rime itself is irreproachable,[5] and the leash which occurs is no more than recurrence of a single rime throughout the course of two staves.[6] Farmer assigned the play to John Heywood,[7] but

[1] Saintsbury, i. 340.

[2] Eckhardt, i. 48.

[3] Except for the contemporary *Robin Conscience* (which may also be considered to consist of cinquains: see p. 57) and *The Conflict of Conscience.* The plays of conscience appear to have stimulated an extraordinary conscientiousness in regard to versification. At this time, too, it is fitting to dispose of misapprehension engendered by the words of Saintsbury (above, n. 1): "Rimes . . . sometimes alternate, sometimes coupled, and sometimes disposed in the quintet or yet more irregular form so often mentioned." Even a rapid perusal of this play will show the reader that the work is in strict form.

[4] 72-73.

[5] The most flagrant rimes are "heryse"/I (138/40) and patient/resistance (880/2).

[6] 477-489.

[7] R. W. Bolwell, *The Life and Works of John Heywood* (New York, 1921), p. 116.

the internal evidence of metrical analysis would negate such opinion. The dearth of unrimed lines, the lower number—by half—of double rimes, and the absence of Heywood's great carry-all (the tetrameter couplet) do not make this interlude appear to be his handiwork.[8]

[8] A summary of the metrical characteristics of Heywood's dramas has the following complexion:

	Rime Royal %	Couplets %	Quatrains %	Polysyllabic rime %
The Four P's:	1.1	96.7	2.3	14.3
John John:	...	97.1	3.0	9.5
Love:	27.0	72.2	.3	8.6
The Pardoner and Friar:	...	64.6	33.4	10.3
The Weather:	16.7	69.2	12.9	14.5
Witty and Witless:	5.0	95.0	...	14.8
Gentleness and Nobility:	6.6	91.0	...	6.0
The Four Elements:	24.7	2.3	3.1	2.5

XVII. (Of) Gentleness and Nobility

Text: J. S. Farmer, ed. (London, 1908).
Date: 1530.[1]
Rhythm: light.
Prevailing metre: tetrameter couplets.

Lines:	1173	%
Dissyllabic rime:	70	6.0
Redundant rime:	3	.3
Identical rime:	6	.5
Latin rime:	4	.3
Rime lacking:	1	.1
Linkage:	2	.2
Tetrameter couplets:	1072	91.0
Tetrameter rime royal:	77	6.6
Leash:	28	2.4

John Heywood has been suggested as the author of this play, and analysis of the versification tends to strengthen such suggestion.[2] Graciously in the manner of *John John* the drama proceeds, and the figures above substantiate the more general aspects of this work. A large body of dissyllabic rime enters with the Plowman.[3] Like *The Play of the Weather, Witty and Witless*, and *The Four P's, Gentleness and Nobility* ends with the light rime royal in tetrameter, and like them is constituted of the light rimed tetrameter to an unusual degree. Dissyllabic rime in all averages more than ten per cent and is so extravagant that it cannot escape notice. From internal evidence alone, seen from the vantage of prosody, *Gentleness and Nobility* so corresponds

[1] Whiting, p. 182.

[2] R. W. Bolwell, *The Life and Works of John Heywood* (New York, 1921), pp. 93-4.

[3] Text, p. 10. The rimes are likewise good as they are in those interludes known to be from Heywood's pen. The strangest of them in this play are place/tools ("tolis"; 55/6).

to the work of Heywood that there should be no hesitation in accounting him its author.[4]

Not until the play is complete does the dramatist deviate from the tetrameter couplets with which he began. The Merchant having finished speaking and an "Amen" indited, the Philosopher speaks an epilogue in eleven stanzas of rime royal, two of which are linked by a common rime. Twelve cases of double rime indicate that he has not put this difficult touchstone of poetic facility behind him. The consequence of such a summary dealing with the question of prosody is to show the extreme consciousness of the playwright of the forms he was using, reserving entirely for the body of his verse the rambling verse, and the solemn seven-lined stanza for the philosophical aftermath.

[4] A. W. Reed, *Early Tudor Drama* (London, 1926), pp. 106-12, has presented evidence in favor of John Rastell's authorship of *Gentleness and Nobility.* Prosodic anlaysis, however, strongly militates against this ascription; for a condensed summary of these metrics, see p. 52, n. 8.

XVIII. John John, Tib, and Sir John[1]

Text: Adams, pp. 385-396.
Date: 1530.[2]
Rhythm: light.
Prevailing metre: tetrameter couplets.

Lines:	678	%
Dissyllabic rime:	62	9.2
Trisyllabic rime:	2	.3
Identical rime:	1	.1
Rime lacking:	3	.4
Tetrameter couplets:	658	97.1
Tetrameter quatrain:	20	3.0

Like *The Pardoner and the Friar*, the present play, which is reasonably ascribed to John Heywood, is written in only light tetrameters which rime for the most part in couplets. The few examples of alternate rime are found sprinkled throughout the text:[3] there is neither prologue nor epilogue (for each would be quite out of place in a comedy as lively as this), and from the very first line the verse tumbles rapidly away. The cases of quatrain which belong to "Syr Johan, the preest" have little in common; they are all on the subject of wedlock, which the good priest is doing his best to rive, and they are scattered about one from another. Their sole purpose seems to be that of varying the inevitable closure of each couplet. The poet's metrics are good, his rimes apt,[4] and his feet typical of the dramatic doggerel which he did so much to establish as the vehicle for the Tudor interlude. A sprightly comedy, any severe alteration in the versification would be out of place, and since there are but three characters in the one scene, the failure of the dramatist to attract attention to the mechanics of his trade is altogether commendable artistically.

[1] Brandl, pp. li-liii.
[2] Eckhardt, i. 45.
[3] 341-344, 497-500, 525-528, 543-546, 581-584.
[4] The most interesting of his rimes are happy/reck I (187/8).

XIX. The Prodigal Son

Text: W. W. Greg, ed., for the Malone Society, "Collections," (London, 1907), I. i. 27-30.
Date: 1530.[1]
Rhythm: light.
Prevailing metre: tetrameter couplets.

Lines:	72	%
Redundant rime:	1	1.4
Rime lacking:[2]	4	5.6
Tetrameter couplets:	30	41.7
Pentameter couplets:	15	20.9
Dimeter couplets:	13	18.1
Sixain coué:	6	8.3
Dimeter quatrain, abba:	4	5.6
Miscellaneous:	11	15.3

The prosody of *The Prodigal Son* might also be called spontaneous. In couplets for the most part, it is so irregular within its small compass with its prose interruptions and repetitions that one is tempted to dismiss it as of inconsequential versification. The "In Memoriam stanza"[3] has no significance in the mouth of "Vxor,"[4] and the rime couée of "Filius"[5] no more illustrates his folly than do the jagged couplets which precede and follow it. Metre, too, is sacrificed on the altar of comedy. To this Muse are offered the Skeltonics of "Servus," devoid as they are of significance.[6] The alliteration of the composition seems to be confined to the names that make up this leash on nine lines.[7] The anonymous author of this scabroüs fragment rimed as he chose and treated the syllables of his verses with the same *nonchaloir*;[8] one cannot say that he had a purpose in the employment of his divers metres.

[1] Text, p. 27.

[2] Three of these belong to a brief prose interruption repeated at intervals (9, 12, 25).

[3] Or "Phoenix and Turtle stanza"; Schipper, ii. 545-7.

[4] 8-11.

[5] 28-33.

[6] 70-80.

[7] 70-78.

[8] In the rime couée, for example, they proceed 886458.

XX. (The Book of) Robin Conscience

Text: J. O. Halliwell, ed., *Contributions to Early English Literature* (London, 1849).
Date: 1530.[1]
Rhythm: light.
Prevailing metre: tetrameter rime royal.

Lines:	312	%
Dissyllabic rime:	40	12.8
Tetrameter rime royal:[2]	312	100.

The peculiar rime royal of *Robin Conscience* points to the writer's preoccupation with the subject of prosody. The last two lines of each stanza are identified with the person who speaks it as a kind of chanting couplet to close the stave. In this case alone does the verse approach the Italian *ottava rima*, but an *ottava rima* whose final couplet acts as a refrain. It is not a perfect refrain, however, for it does change from time to time, at the end of each scene.[3] The chief point of interest is the particular construction of this stanza with its alternation of *differentiae* according to the speaker.[4]

The author's originality in the construction of his stanzas does not extend to his treatment of the whole question of prosody. For the entire compass of his play he has used the one measure of his fashioning, this rime royal with alternation of caudal lines. One therefore concludes that prosody is a matter of major interest in *Robin Conscience*—although once the pattern has been adopted, no variation alters it—that the novelty of the system which the poet adopted kept his interest in the metrics of the *débat* alive, and that he was at pains to foster the method he had conceived.

[1] Eckhardt, i. 25.

[2] Of a most particular kind, riming ababbCC. In 187 Robin alters the last word of his *differentia* without affecting the rime.

[3] Following 65 and 187.

[4] There is an exceptional use of internal rime in some of these concluding couplets; whether it is accidental or not is difficult to say. In the first hemistich of each couplet in the position of refrain after 199/200 the phenomenon reappears. It is similar to the internal rime of *Common Conditions*: see p. 159, n. 4.

XXI. Temperance and Humility

Text: W. W. Greg, ed., for the Malone Society, "Collections," (London, 1909) I. iii. 245-246.
Date: 1530.[1]
Rhythm: light.
Alliteration: marked.
Prevailing metre: tetrameter quatrains.

Lines:	62	%
Redundant rime:	3	4.8
Rime lacking:	1	1.6
Tetrameter quatrains:	16	25.8
Tetrameter couplets:	12	19.4
Tetrameter neuvain coué:	9	14.5
Pentameter rime royal:	7	11.3
Tetrameter sixain coué:	6	9.7
Miscellaneous:[2]	10	16.1

Except for the *grotesquerie* where the fragment breaks off,[2] the riming of this play falls into well-defined patterns, varied as they are. Disobedience speaks first with dignity in the five-beat rime royal,[3] later cutting his phrase to four beats;[4] of the whole company he alone uses this measure. Temperance, on the contrary, a character seemingly of good faith, speaks in the rime couée, and Disobedience follows suit.[5] It is the temptation of Temperance and Humility which incurs this metre. Disobedience, unsuccessful in his effort to beguile the forces of good, allows himself to be drawn into their vortex of couplets and quatrains, these being the vehicles of virtue triumphant.[6]

The short extant bit of this *débat* does not show definite

[1] Text, p. 243.
[2] The rime scheme of the last ten lines approximates ababbbccdd.
[3] 3-9.
[4] 12-18.
[5] 17-31. The two metres overlap, but the tailed system is apparently the one desired.
[6] 32-62.

conscious use of the various metres but seems rather to use them as most convenient. The syllables are not of a regularity,[7] particularly in the rime couée and toward the end, where the lines grow longer and longer. The versification is slipshod; the author cannot be thought to have taken particular pains to identify situation or character with a definite scheme of rimes.

It may be that the increasing attention paid to alliteration caused him to disregard a studied versification. This element is not sufficiently pronounced to warrant the lapse of judgment that occurs at the end, where the lines rime as they please, nor is there any consistency in the application of alliterating words. These too link themselves as well as they may, and one reaches the conclusion that there is no more thought or forethought connected with the notion of "head-rime" than with that of true rime.

[7] In 19-22 the number of syllables is respectively 4, 13, 9+, and 6. Line 21 is acephalous.

XXII. Wit and Science[1]

Text: Adams, pp. 325-342.
Date: 1530.[2]
Rhythm: light.
Prevailing metre: tetrameter couplets.

Lines:	1020	%
Dissyllabic rime:	209	20.5
Trisyllabic rime:	6	.6
Redundant rime:	1	.1
Rime lacking:	3	.3
Prose:[3]	90	8.8
Tetrameter couplets:	825	80.8
Dimeter couplets:	34	3.3
Dimeter quatrain:	32	3.1
Dimeter sixain coué:	30	2.9
Pentameter rime royal:	7	.7

The interlude of John Redford shows comparative diversity of metrical form. Even a sort of prose appears in one of the scenes, that of the lowest comedy, in which Ignorance and Idleness divert the audience with the former's folly: a typical vice-scene.[3] The torso of the play, however, is in the dramatic doggerel, beginning with this measure and carrying through to the end.[4] Light rime royal by Reason concludes the dramatic portion,[5] and a song completes the performance. The verse is satisfactory, for there are few of the usual aberrations from the set structure.

Hemistich quatrains after the manner of John Skelton come into the play with the entrance of Tediousness, a vice

[1] Brandl, p. lxi.

[2] Text, p. 325.

[3] 453-542.

[4] A page or so has been lost at the beginning of the manuscript, and the play must necessarily be considered as commencing with the rimed tetrameters, although the verse-form of the prologue—and there probably was a prologue—is not, like the Sirens' song, beyond all conjecture. Its form was perhaps that of the tail-piece, rime royal.

[5] 1094-1100.

who wears a "vyser" and bears a club.[6] As a personality, he is anything but tedious, and the alternate rime of his half-lines[7] enhances the life and comic color he brings to the moral hebetude of the preceding scene.[8] As the enthusiasm of Tediousness for his prospective pleasure in thwacking Wit waxes, he dispenses with the alternate rime and settles into true Skeltonics,[9] the dimeter couplets of *Philip Sparrow* and *The Tunning of Eleanor Rumming*. When the Vice has finished with the metametric "Ho, ho! ho, ho!" Wit enters, is beaten, and is resuscitated by Honest Recreation. For several lines they make use again of the rimed dimeter when the philandering Wit attempts to steal a kiss from his nurse.[10] The verse moves swiftly into rime couée when a dance is suggested and anticipated.[11] Henceforward the metre remains the tumbling verse with which our portion of the fragment begins.[12]

John Redford, organist and composer, attuned his ear to the various metres in use among his contemporaries, and he intended to profit by their example. He began with a systematic use of form, but his lack of poetical facility turned him from his purpose before the interlude was one-third complete. His trouble with rime is soon noticed,[13] and although he set himself steadfastly to procure rimes for his dramatic doggerel, his lapse into prose is virtually unique in the early history of the interlude. Variation in prosody, however, was always in the musician's mind; when he forsook the earlier variety of hemistichic verse, he reserved poetical schemes for his songs and for his epilogue, and his consciousness of the styles of versification did not faint.

[6] After 140. This whole passage in dimeter looks like a song. Although there are no directions so to take it, there is more reason for considering its aspect lyrical than, for instance, the Skeltonic portion of Heywood's *Play of Love* (text, 425-464); see p. 63, n. 3.

[7] 141-168.

[8] Between Instruction and other virtues with Wit (1-140).

[9] 169-192.

[10] 287-296.

[11] 301-330. A quatrain which they share intervenes (297-300).

[12] Except, of course, for the two songs (626-639, 986-1015).

[13] Especially in the song "Exceeding Measure" (626-639).

XXIII. Redford Fragment, 1.

Text: J. O. Halliwell, ed., for the Shakespeare Society (London, 1848), p. 55.
Date: 1530.[1]
Rhythm: light.
Prevailing metre: tetrameter couplets.

Lines:	10	%
Dissyllabic rime:	2	20.0
Tetrameter couplets:	10	100.

Redford Fragment, 2.

Text: ibid., p. 73.
Date: 1530.[1]
Rhythm: light.
Prevailing metre: tetrameter quatrain.[2]

Lines:	8	%
Rime lacking:	4	50.0
Tetrameter quatrain:[2]	8	100.

These two stray bits of John Redford's work have never merited attention. The first of them is accurately turned into its riming tetrameters, but the second, short as it is, is so deficient in rime that it is hard to classify.[2] They are too small to be of interest; one merely notes their existence and proceeds. If they can show anything, it is that the Tudor interlude continues to spin down the grooves of the light tetrameter, particularly when paired. The lesser frequency of alternate rime is borne out even in this brief space.

[1] Conjecturally supplied from that of *Wit and Science*, p. 60.

[2] In so far as it can be pigeon-holed. The rimes are actually more in the nature of *terza rima* (abacdefe) but were probably intended for two quatrains.

XXIV. The Play of Love[1]

Text: Brandl, pp. 159-209.
Date: 1533.[2]
Rhythm: light.
Prevailing metre: tetrameter couplets.

Lines:[3]	1533	%
Dissyllabic rime:	132	7.7
Redundant rime:	3	.2
Rime lacking:	4	.3
Tetrameter couplets:	1106	72.2
Tetrameter rime royal:	372	24.2
Pentameter rime royal:	42	2.8
Tetrameter quatrain:	4	.3
Miscellaneous:	7	.5

As if there were a prologue, the drama begins in rime royal when the three flawed lovers discourse on the theme of the play,[4] and to them enters Lover Beloved.[5] No Lover Nor Loved comes in to make merry on the same subject in couplets,[6] into which Lover Beloved is once permitted to break with his Chaucerian measure.[7] The play carries on in the dramatic doggerel until the end is in sight,[8] but it is broken up at various intervals by the appearance of rime royal with the words of Lover Beloved,[9] and later Loved Not Loving.[10] These two bring the "contentacyon" to its "Amen" with similarly philosophical observations in rime royal.[11]

[1] Text, pp. li-liii; Bond, p. lxxxiv; Reyher, p. 59.
[2] Eckhardt, i. 45.
[3] The forty lines of Skeltonics (425-464) are considered as song, following the precedent of R. Bell in *Songs from the Dramatists* (New York, 1882), pp. 23-4.
[4] 1-245.
[5] 245-301.
[6] 302-319.
[7] 320-327.
[8] 302-1538.
[9] 689-702, 1455-1461 (this in lines of five stresses), 1478-1484.
[10] 1492-1525, 1530-1536.
[11] In pentameter: 1539-1573.

The system by which John Heywood alternated rime royal with tumbling verse is apparent. For the more abstract of the speeches concerning love, most like those of the *débats*, he utilized the ballad measure of seven lines for the sake of dignity; whereas for the more humorous scenes, in which love is treated dispassionately, he is content to let the verse tumble as it will. The breaks in the above tides are infrequent and fall into the large divisions noted. Although by volume there is three times as much doggerel as rime royal, the playwright is seen to have been careful of both and to have used each with consideration.

XXV. The Play of the Weather[1]

Text: Adams, pp. 397-419.
Date: 1533.[2]
Rhythm: light.
Prevailing metre: tetrameter couplets.

Lines:	1254	%
Dissyllabic rime:	178	14.2
Trisyllabic rime:	4	.3
Redundant rime:	1	.1
Rime lacking:	5	.4
Tetrameter couplets:	868	69.2
Pentameter rime royal:	210	16.7
Tetrameter quatrain:	162	12.9
Trimeter octave couée:	8	.6
Dimeter octave couée:	8	.6

"The Play of the Wether" is the only one of John Heywood's interludes to show great internal variation in metre with conscious attempts to fit it to the speaker. There are three main types of verse: rime royal, quatrains, and couplets;[3] and they are used with fine discrimination. According to the standards of verse in the interlude, the metrical work in the present play is well done.

Jupiter from his throne speaks the prologue and epilogue in rime royal of four and five stresses, hendecasyllabics predominating. After Jupiter's prefatory words Merry-Report, interlocutor, genial vice, and manifestation of Heywood's *vis comica,* enters to hold parley with the King in tumbling verse.[4] He states the case for those who later appear in the course of the play, and Jupiter replies in rime royal.[5] Couplets return for the language of the scene of the Gentleman, seeking admittance, and Merry-Report, acting the intercessor.[6] To Jupiter

[1] Brandl, p. lii; Reyher, p. 52, n.

[2] Eckhardt, i. 44.

[3] The sixteen lines of tail-rime (1057-1064, 1139-1146) play no dramatic or personable rôle in the drama.

[4] 99-100, 175-178.

[5] 161-174, 179-185.

[6] 186-257.

himself the Gentleman presents his brief in quatrains,[7] and he is answered in rime royal.[8] Tumbling verse supervenes until the Merchant asks his favor of the monarch in alternate rime.[9] The Water-miller[10] and the Launderer[11] are privileged to speak in the long measure, too, but Merry-Report keeps the Wind-miller, the Gentlewoman, and the others down to his own plane of the dramatic doggerel. When the various applicants have been heard by Jupiter, Merry-Report makes a proclamation to the audience in rime couée.[12] Later, when he brings the "sewters" back on-stage to hear the sage verdict of Jupiter in rime royal,[13] he chants or sings a few more lines of rime couée.[14] The various plaintiffs hear the decision of Jupiter as just, and in quatrains and couplets acquiesce. The Gentleman and the Merchant reply in the quatrains;[15] dramatic doggerel suffices for the Ranger, Water-miller, and those who had previously used it in applying to their sovereign.[16]

The manner in which Heywood altered his versification is therefore apparent and significant. For the words of Jupiter *ex cathedrâ* he uses rime royal, for the suits of his more important applicants he uses alternate rime, and for scenes dominated by the spalpeen of the piece, Merry-Report, the light rimed tetrameter provides the carrier. The result is a studied attempt to fit the verse to the character, to suit royalty with rime royal, and so on. However it may detract from the dramatic interest in this play, it serves accurately to differentiate one character from another as if each were speaking a different language. Change in prosody is forthright and well defined, and indicates the interest the author took in varying it to fit the situation of who speaks the verse.

[7] 258-277.
[8] 278-284.
[9] 345-375.
[10] 442-469.
[11] 966-969.
[12] 1057-1064.
[13] 1155-1210.
[14] 1139-1146.
[15] 1211-1222.
[16] 1223-1240.

XXVI. A Satire of the Three Estates[1]

Text: D. Laing, ed., *The Poetical Works of Sir David Lyndsay* (Edinburgh, 1879. 3 vols.), ii. 11-222.
Date: 1535.[2]
Rhythm: heavy.
Alliteration: marked.
Prevailing metre: pentameter couplets.

Lines:	4570	%
Dissyllabic rime:	175	3.8
Redundant rime:	1	..
Identical rime:	2	..
Internal rime:	9	.2
Latin rime:	14	.3
Unrimed Latin:	3	.1
Rime lacking:[3]	5	.1
Prose:[4]	82	1.8
Pentameter couplets:	886	19.4
Tetrameter couplets:	861	18.8
Tetrameter octave couée:	717	15.7
Trimeter sixain coué:	636	13.9
Pentameter ballad-eight:	560	12.3
Tetrameter ballad-eight:	415	9.0
Tetrameter quatrain:[3]	95	2.1
Pentameter rime royal:	70	1.5
Hexameter couplets:	52	1.1
Common measure:	28	.6
Short measure:	28	.6
Tetrameter ballad-eight with envoi:[5]	26	.6
Trimeter quatrain:	24	.5
Pentameter quatrain:	12	.3
Miscellaneous:[6]	160	3.5

[1] Strictly, "One Satire of the Three Estates"; cf. King James' *Ane Schort Treatise* . . . (p. 12, n. 47). For prosodic commentary on the present interlude see T. F. Henderson, *Scottish Vernacular Literature* (London, 1898), p. 220; Saintsbury, i. 278; Schipper, i. 522-37; Schröer, pp. 236-7, 256-64.

[2] Text, p. 3.

[3] Including two stanzas of Latin (see p. 75, n. 124).

[4] See below, n. 88.

[5] For want of a better name this queer five-line appendage of two and three beats (riming deeed by being linked to the preceding ballad-

The giant among interludes, so long that the court of the Scottish King James V. sat for nine hours during its presentation in 1535,[2] contains in its extraordinary compass a variety of metres. These include the unusual "Burns measure"[7] and the kyrielle[8] in addition to the stock of rimes couées and more usual ballad measures and couplets. Since the only important specimen of the early Scottish drama has never been analyzed to determine the various structures of which it is composed, it will be necessary to append such an analysis in order that the prosodic significance of the different particles be understood.

The "Pleasant Satyre" commences with the highly alliterative words of Diligence in the thirteen-line strophe[9] that has already been encountered in *The World and the Child*.[10] The coda drops off after a pause, and he continues in the ballad-eight as harbinger of the drama.[11] Octave couée diverts him as he speaks of the evil things which are to be observed and the various abuses which must be rectified;[12] but when he intones a warning unto the nation, he reverts to

eight stave) is called by that of a French analogue. Of the Provençal *mieja canso* or *tornada* with its *senhal* there is no sign. It appears only a coincidence that the Scot added the half-strophe to a ballad-eight, which was the Continental practice (see *Las Leys d'amors,* ed. J. Anglade [Paris, 1919-20. 4 vols.] ii. 176).

[6] Consisting of incomplete rimes couées aaabab (482-487: the Burns measure; see below, n. 7) and of variants in the ballad schemes: abbcbc (1250-1255), ababcccc (1552-1560), etc.

[7] The stanza of various characteristic poems of Robert Burns, e.g. *To a Mouse, To a Louse,* and *Scotch Drink.* See Schipper, ii. 586-7. In the present case, however, it may be only an incomplete rime couée; see above, n. 6.

[8] A quatrain (aabb or abab) whose last line acts as a refrain, being repeated from stanza to stanza; see J. C. Parsons, *English Versification* (Boston, 1891), p. 120. Henderson (above, n. 1) has recognized its presence here; he gives no indication where.

[9] See p. 67, n. 5.

[10] See p. 22, n. 3. In the earlier interlude it is linked by rime to what precedes, but that is not the case here (1-13).

[11] 14-29.

[12] 30-45.

the linked quatrains.[13] The populace is addressed in rime couée,[14] and Rex Humanitas enters with the dignified ballad-eight.[15] Wantonness interrupts his prayer with insidious proposals for pleasure, using the tailed octave and thicker dialect,[16] and the "vice scene" that follows carries on the same measure.[17] The king resists their advances in the treizain[18] with which diligence began the play, but Placebo, a vice, keeps up the attack, abetted by the others.[19] Wantonness varies the verse with a ballad stave[20] while Sensuality in compelling phrases and ballad octaves proposes to seek Dame Venus.[21] Lyric measures then follow (although there is no direction to sing),[22] and the king wonders what is going on. The vicious element continues its destructive work in tail-rime[23] which is at times riven by couplets[24] and ballad staves,[25] the king too lapsing into the familiar rime couée[26] and the Burns measure.[27] Wantonness continues his maleficence in heroic couplets,[28] and Sensuality, with two stanzas of rime royal,[29] some rime couée,[30] and alliteration, assists him.[31] Rex Humanitas yields ground slowly in long measure[32] as the vices press their work in linked quatrains.[33]

[13] 46-69.
[14] 70-77.
[15] 78-101.
[16] 100-117.
[17] 118-213.
[18] 214-226.
[19] 227-270.
[20] 235-242.
[21] 271-287.
[22] 295-310.
[23] 337-360.
[24] 417-438, 447-450.
[25] 439-446.
[26] 361-392, 406-409.
[27] Merely its variant, 482-487.
[28] 488-494.
[29] 500-513.
[30] 514-526.
[31] 527-535.
[32] 531-534.
[33] 547-554.

Good Counsel appeals for divine assistance in the ballad octave of five stresses,[34] and then speaks to whoever will listen, in rime couée[35]—as if turning from the heavens to the earth: such is the ratio between ballad measure and tail-rime. Flattery uses a syncopated cinquain coué[36] and couplets,[37] while Deceit speaks in the tailed octave.[38] The vices continue their pernicious activity in couplets[39] and ballad octave,[40] reverting to the waist-and-tailed stanzas briefly,[41] only, probably, to draw attention to the long rimes of Falsity. As the vices have their way and engage Good Counsel, whom the king has rejected, in conversation, couplets are their vehicle, some of four[42] and some of five beats.[43] It is Verity who restores ballad-eights to the drama in rebuking the king.[44] Ecclesiastical characters employ alternate rime in their encounter with the iniquitous and accomplish the undeserved punishment of Verity.[45] Couplets intervene for a short time in the complaints of the unhappy virtues,[46] but their true medium is the eight-line ballad measure.[47] The clerical prototypes, under the spell of vice, use the vicious tail-rime;[48] a short span of couplets for the gabbling of women permits them to drive off Chastity.[49] When they have gone, the taint of their vulgarity remains behind in the rime couée they have bequeathed to Diligence and Chastity.[50] Ballad-eights

[34] 555-570.
[35] 571-594.
[36] 603-637.
[37] 646-649, 652-658.
[38] 659-688.
[39] 689-839, 849-888.
[40] 840-848.
[41] 889-904.
[42] 955-988, 995-1020, 1025-1036.
[43] 989-994, 1021-1024.
[44] 1038-1084.
[45] 1085-1183.
[46] 1184-1199.
[47] 1200-1223, 1226-1255.
[48] 1256-1307.
[49] 1308-1341.
[50] 1396-1411.

supervene as the ill-adverted Rex Humanitas, Sensuality, and Discretion speak;[51] but Chastity, like Verity, in the stocks bewails the turn of things in tail-rime.[52] Verity speaks in linked quatrains[53] and is interrupted by Correction's Varlet with more tail-rime.[54] The vices thus gloat over what they have done[55] and, when they have stolen the king's box, speak in alternate rime.[56] Divine Correction then takes over the dramatic reins in ballad-eights,[57] and thus does Good Counsel bid him welcome after his long soliloquy.[58] The ladies being fetched from the stocks, they proceed toward the king; and the vices rail at each other in tail-rime.[59] In Monk's Tale stanzas Correction intones reveille,[60] the drama moving on in linked quatrains. Sensuality leaves the king with rime couée,[61] and after a singing trimeter quatrain of Spirituality,[62] Correction speaks to the king severely in ballad measure.[63] His plain language takes the form of even rime couée to make sure that he is understood,[64] and in such earthy mold the succeeding scene between Correction, Diligence, and the king is cast.[65] The female virtues speak in ballad-eights.[66] Good Counsel brings the first half of the drama to its conclusion with heroic couplets,[67] Diligence, the messenger, alone following her in quatrains[68] in order to

[51] 1412-1451.
[52] 1452-1473.
[53] 1474-1481.
[54] 1482-1515.
[55] 1516-1551.
[56] 1552-1578.
[57] 1580-1627.
[58] 1628-1653; 1636-1637 are an interruption of Correction.
[59] 1676-1699.
[60] 1700-1739.
[61] 1740-1747.
[62] 1748-1751.
[63] 1752-1759.
[64] 1760-1775.
[65] 1784-1857. Rex Humanitas, before embracing Correction (following 1775), speaks a stave of ballad-eight.
[66] 1860-1881.
[67] 1882-1907.
[68] 1908-1923.

send the audience home to get something to eat. He further advises them, in rime couée,[69] not to surfeit themselves, for the better half is yet to come.

Part II begins with the interlude of "The Puir Man and the Pardoner." Pentameter couplets[70] soon give way to couplets of an exceptional raggedness, which is due to the quantity of alliteration they contain.[71] The stresses cannot be discerned; sometimes there are six, or more often seven. The closest link one can find is to the work of John Bale, for the present dodecasyllabics bear a near relationship to the "Alexandrines" of the Bishop[72] and to those of *Respublica.*[73] Tail-rime returns as the Pardoner airs his theology.[74] The action of the drama then reaches its nadir in couplets[75] that pass to more rime couée.[76] The mephitic *intermezzo* is concluded in consecutive rime,[77] and Diligence proclaims the commencement of the second part in ballad-eights.[78] Back come the vices with their tailed doggerel,[79] Good Counsel following their lead.[80] The three Estates—Spirituality, Temporality, and "Merchand"—speak to the king in rime royal[81] in parliamentary wise, and he replies to them in a ballad octave.[82] Couplets follow with the remonstrances of the Estates,[83] lengthening in the words of John the Commonweal,[84] and reverting to long measure in the speech of the

[69] 1924-1931.

[70] 1932-1943.

[71] In particular 1944-1959, although the couplets go through to the unrimed Latin line 2042; see Schröer, pp. 240, 256.

[72] See p. 90.

[73] See p. 112.

[74] 2043-2125.

[75] 2174-2183.

[76] 2184-2219. Wilkin speaks a tetrameter quatrain (2220-2223).

[77] 2224-2297.

[78] 2298-2319.

[79] 2320-2343.

[80] 2344-2355.

[81] 2356-2376.

[82] 2395-2402.

[83] 2403-2420.

[84] 2421-2422, 2428-2430, 2448-2470.

Sergeants of the Law as they take the vices off to the stocks.[85] Covetousness restores couplets of five beats,[86] which shrink, with the Estates, to tetrameters.[87] They become the vehicle for parliamentary discussion in what proves to be the most sustained passage in the play from the prosodic standpoint. Even the Latin prose[88] and its translation does not interrupt the flood of couplets; only when Verity and Chastity make their complaint at the bar in the cause of Spirituality does the metre change to linked quatrains.[89] Couplets are resumed as a matter of convenience when the Scribe, Tailor, and Suitor are each granted but one line.[90] Good Counsel and the others follow the bourgeois example, and Diligence departs.[91] Temporality with an oath pleads in Monk's Tale stanzas[92] for compassion on the clerical profession when, like a bombshell, Common Theft bursts in among them with tail-rime.[93] Beguiled into sitting in the stocks, he is disposed of, and the metre is permitted to return to couplets.[94] Divine Correction hails the Doctor in ballad-eights[95] that Spirituality follows with heroic couplets.[96] But for sporadic interruption,[97] the scene goes along in couplets[98] until the Doctor ascends to the pulpit and preaches in ballad octaves on death and redemption.[99] The Abbot speaks likewise, but the Parson, enraged, attempts to bait the Doctor in octaves of alternate rime which have a tendency toward Skeltonics.[100]

[85] 2479-2496.
[86] 2503-2516.
[87] 2517-2552 and following.
[88] 2912.
[89] 3104-3131.
[90] 3140-3143.
[91] 3149-3181.
[92] 3182-3197.
[93] 3201-3209, 3211-3261.
[94] 3262-3321.
[95] 3338-3353.
[96] 3363-3388.
[97] A ballad-eight intervenes (3397-3404).
[98] 3361-3452.
[99] 3460-3522.
[100] 3541-3551.

The disputation between the licentiates and the bachelor on matters religious in couplets[101] is superseded by the words of the bachelor alone, which in a state of flux pass gradually from the ballad-eight[102] to the rime couée *en six*.[103] The police take Flattery, garbed like a friar, into custody and bestow him in the stocks before the ballad measures are restored.[104] These should have eight lines, but an occasional one is omitted.[105] "Parliament" carries on in couplets[106] which turn to rime royal when John the Commonweal becomes an M.P.[107] The ballad measure of seven lines[108] becomes expanded to that of eight when the Scribe proclaims the Fifteen Acts of Parliament.[109] The Pauper voices his approval in tumbling verse,[110] which also serves for the hanging of the prisoners.[111] Deceit has much to say in tail-rime before they have done with him, and so has Falsity.[112] Falsity's last remarks, however, are in couplets,[113] but the pleasure of Flattery returns in rime couée.[114]

The fourth section of the *Satire* is the "Sermon of Folly."[115] It begins in rime couée,[116] which Rex Humanitas alters to tumbling verse.[117] The rich Scottish dialect which the vices imported before they were hanged abides in the

[101] 3572-3601.

[102] 3602-3613.

[103] 3614-3659.

[104] 3626-3653, 3660-3697.

[105] Thus the sequence 3784-3790 is converted into rime royal. A b-rime is omitted from the octave in 3932-3938. The ballad stanzas run from 3784 to 3962.

[106] 3724-3783.

[107] 3784-3803.

[108] 3804-3962.

[109] 3963-3978.

[110] 3979-4026.

[111] 4030-4098.

[112] 4105-4212.

[113] 4213-4252.

[114] 4253-4322. With 4282, however, Flattery ceases to speak.

[115] 4283-4652.

[116] 4283-4322.

[117] 4323-4374.

language of Folly, who turns to tail-rime again[118] for a short time until his stichomythy with Diligence proves prelude to more tumbling verse.[119] Folly, with "bum, baleriebum, bum," entices Diligence back into rime couée,[120] which Diligence must again raise to the level of rimed tetrameters.[121] The long-awaited sermon on "Stultorum numerus infinitus" now begins in tumbling fours,[122] and when its three sections are complete, the metre remains the same to conclude the drama.[123] "Ane ill savorit dische" of mediæval Latin in the mouth of Folly is intercalated here[124] before the satire comes to its extremity with two stanzas of ballad octaves by Diligence,[125] an address of pious exhortation to the audience, and one of octave couée to bring the day's entertainment rudely back to earth and tavern.[126]

For all the elaboration of prosodic materials which went into the great interlude, diverse and rich as they were, the threads which bind them together are not too fine for observation. Rime couée seems generally to have been used for scenes in which vice played the most prominent part, and in this there is no departure from the unspoken canon of the ancestral Medwall. For the scenes of greater dignity, for those in which the virtues bear the sway, ballad measures are chiefly invoked, and this too is directly in the tradition. Obviously it is not the measure of seven lines but that of eight which the Scottish jurist liked to use; even in the

[118] 4375-4382.

[119] 4383-4386.

[120] 4387-4394.

[121] 4395-4410; alternate rime is found in 4471-4482.

[122] 4483-4526.

[123] 4527-4628.

[124] 4609-4616. This entrée is particularly noteworthy as the only specimen of mediæval Latin poetry which has come as such into the Tudor interlude. By a kind of irony it is to be discovered in a play of tetraploid proportions stemming from Edinburgh; see p. 194. The great Scottish Latinists like Barclay, Buchanan, and others will be recalled in this connexion; see J. H. Millar, *A Literary History of Scotland* (New York, 1903), pp. 145-51, 244-6.

[125] 4629-4644.

[126] 4645-4652.

scenes in which the king speaks the playwright eschews deliberately the use of rime royal—however it may have been anointed by his own sovereign of an earlier date in the *Kingis Quhair*[127]—in favor of the ballad octave.[128] Couplets, in general, were considered a kind of third-class vehicle for the transportation of ideas, and although exception may with justice be taken to this notion, couplets were useful mostly as foils to rime couée. Corollary to the item of closed rime, i.e. couplet, there is open rime, or quatrain: this measure, when not formed by the slight disintegration of the ballad-eight, is put into passages of couplets for the sake of variety. Common measure and short measure serve their purposes of variety, perhaps of lyrical variety. The Burns measure, a rarity that has found employment in verse previous to this time (but not in the drama), grants one but a glimpse, as if it were another jewel decking the royal state. The envoi or coda, whether or not inherited, remains a *tic* of the author, an idiosyncratic atavistical enigma.

From the medley of metres in the *Satire of the Three Estates* one must conclude that Sir David Lindsay was conscious of his prosodic materials almost to excess. Refinement is exquisite in the application of metres if not in the details of their construction. Nor is the verse bad: it is surprisingly better than that of nearly all other interludes, including those written by others of the learned professions. The various forms of poetry are used with a purpose and a method superior to that of the English playwrights—writers of interludes—who preceded and who followed him. Fifteen hundred and thirty-five was still early in the age of the interlude (in this case "Stuart interlude"), and the *Satire* is in many ways its apogee. The ever-changing metres must have taxed the author considerably, for he knew he must nourish his behemoth on a variety of fare. It is difficult to praise this work too much, for its length set many obstacles; and that its verse continues always to be interesting in its manifold variations, each not only equal but superior

[127] About 1423 by James I.

[128] Attention is especially focussed on 3784-3962.

to the work of contemporaries in the field, contributes to make it the bipartite *Faust* among interludes.[129] Like Goethe, the similarly versatile Sir David was thoroughly awake to his versification, and he became a master of it.

[129] In the variety of its measures, in the diversity of its thought, in the greater cerebral element of the second part, in the increasing abstraction and more intellectual dramatic treatment of concrete things—even in the fact of

Das Ewig-Weibliche
Zieht uns hinan—

one finds close connexion.

XXVII. Thersites[1]

Text: F. J. Child, ed., *Four Old Plays* (Cambridge, 1848), pp. 53-88.
Date: 1537.[2]
Rhythm: light.
Prevailing metre: tetrameter couplets.

Lines:	916	%
Dissyllabic rime:	118	12.9
Redundant rime:	28	3.1
Identical rime:	1	.1
Rime lacking:	1	.1
Tetrameter couplets:	651	70.1
Dimeter couplets:	55	6.0
Trimeter couplets:	53	5.8
Tetrameter quatrain:	44	4.8
Dimeter sixain coué:	42	4.6
Pentameter couplets:	36	3.9
Tetrameter rime royal:	21	2.3
Dimeter quatrain:[3]	8	.8
Tetrameter ballad-six:	6	.6
Miscellaneous:[4]	10	1.1

The rough doggerel of *Thersites* shows little system. *Incipit comoedia* in three stanzas of the light rime royal when Thersites introduces himself, passing from the more elaborate stanza through a tetrametric quatrain[5] to the ordinary dramatic doggerel, where the play is content to rest.[6] He and Mulciber (Vulcan) anvil the verse into Skeltonics at intervals,[7] occasionally varying the procedure with rime that alternates.[8] Without any apparent reason the lines go from

[1] Bond, p. lxxxv; Brandl, p. lxi; Saintsbury, i. 341.
[2] Eckhardt, i. 49.
[3] Riming abab (881-884) and abba (62-65).
[4] Consisting mainly of leash of two and three stresses (453-458).
[5] 22-25.
[6] 25-56 and following.
[7] 57-65, 78-83, 204-210, etc.
[8] 168-171, 120-123, 885-888.

four to two stresses.[9] The normal verse of four beats in moments of dramatic importance to the playwright (i.e. when peace, after a brief squabble, has returned,[10] or when Mater bids the hero farewell[11]) is diminished to that of three. The terror of the "boester's" mother at the prospect of being beaten by her son makes good use of the hemistich;[12] but it is hard to discover an intimacy of connexion between the unstable length of the lines which rime, the large amount of redundancy and harping on one rime, and the subject of the play.

There is also a slight amount of rime couée, "rym dogerel." The first of it is given to Thersites, who boasts of his ability to lay about him with his club.[13] The heavy character of the verse might well be given emphasis in speaking that would reduce it to a kind of war-chant, which would produce a desirable dramatic effect. The second time the boaster uses it, it is to terrify his mother with the thought of cudgelling her;[14] the effect is the same as it had been before. When last it appears, it is again the prelude to battle, and Miles, like a warrior of the time to which he belongs, clarions his challenge before engaging Thersites.[15]

The elastic verse of this somewhat unpleasant interlude cannot firmly be taken in the grasp of a strait prosody. It is continually varying in length; what remains constant is the desire to write couplets. Alternate rime appears gratuitously and without import.[16] The sole true variation from the norm of couplets, save in the introductory passage of rime royal, is in the tail-rime which the embattled Thersites

[9] 350-452, 459-527. The short lines begin at 528.

[10] 593-609.

[11] 762-763.

[12] 621-626.

[13] 156-167.

[14] 326-349.

[15] 875-880.

[16] What is called in the statistical summary "ballad-six" is a group of tetrameters riming ababbb (120-125). It is at the beginning of Thersites' soliloquy in which he admires his physique. The verse thereafter tumbles away in the dramatic doggerel.

and Miles employ. It is a kind of war-cry or haro. With this sole excursion into the older ways of versifying, *Thersites* is written altogether in the rime that was easiest to write, and the composition bears full witness to the lack of cerebration with which the interlude was hammered together.[17]

[17] The suggestion of Udall's authorship (A. R. Moon, "Was Nicholas Udall the Author of 'Thersites'?" *Library* [1927], IV. vii. 184-93) is not corroborated by the metric analysis: see p. 125, n. 3.

XXVIII. (A Comedy concerning) Three Laws[1]

Text: Schröer, pp. 160-225.
Date: 1538.[2]
Rhythm: heavy.
Prevailing metre: pentameter couplets.

Lines:	2081	%
Dissyllabic rime:	246	11.8
Trisyllabic rime:	4	.2
Redundant rime:	19	1.0
Identical rime:	5	.2
Latin rime:	4	.2
Unrimed Latin:	5	.2
Rime lacking:	3	.1
Prose:[3]	4	.2
Pentameter couplets:	775	37.3
Pentameter rime royal:	362	17.4
Trimeter sixain coué:	292	14.0
Trimeter octave couée:	233	11.2
Tetrameter octave couée:	128	6.7
Tetrameter couplets:	146	7.7
Dimeter sixain coué:	96	4.6
Trimeter neuvain coué:	9	.4
Miscellaneous:[4]	22	1.1

The dramatic work of John Bale, Bishop of Ossory, is strangely uneven in prosody. The first of his interludes here to be discussed is the *Comedy concerning Three Laws*, in which a great diversity of metre is present, but which falls easily into the schemes of rime royal, rime couée, and couplets. The prose is merely a chant with which Infidelitas enters, crying "Broom, broom!"[3] an interruption in the verse that soon is lost in the riming tetrameter that follows.

[1] Text, pp. 238-64; Brandl, p. lxi; Reyher, p. 59.

[2] Eckhardt, i. 27.

[3] Between 177 and 178.

[4] These are for the most part liberties, redundancies, taken with the sixes and eights coués in the first 500 lines, e.g. the group aaaabccddeffegge (225-240) embracing a neuvain coué.

The author—Balaeus Prolocutor—and Deus Pater open the play in rime royal that is now light, now heavy.[5] The three Lexes speak in heroic couplets to the end of Act I, interrupted by rime royal when they all join together.[6] Naturae Lex begins Act II also in the Chaucerian strophe,[7] but when Infidelitas comes in, the verse falls apart into a form of rime doggerel.[8] The drama is furthered in this measure; Naturae Lex breaks in upon it in rime royal[9] only to be superseded later in rimed pentapodies by Moseh[10] Lex (now) Corrupta with Infidelitas.[11] A briefer couplet interrupts, too,[12] but it is of no significance, and the doggerel stanzas come and go.[13] Avaritia, who speaks in the octave couée of three stresses,[14] is distinguished from Ambition, who speaks in the sixain coué of two beats.[15] Infidelitas is different from both of them with his very light tetrameter couplets.[16] But this scheme with its sharp lines of cleavage is not kept up; after the passages of stichomythia[17] Avaritia is capable of five-beat rime royal,[18] while the rest bandy words in the pentameter couplets. Infidelitas in doggerel rime[19] makes way for Moseh Lex to end the third act in rime royal.[20] Evangelium, compassed round by vice, opens the fourth act in rime royal,[21] but his companions soon pull it

[5] 1-56. Bale's *morae* are always hard to account for.

[6] 63-104.

[7] 164-177.

[8] 184-743.

[9] 744-792.

[10] The Ephraimite reading of the ש is consistent.

[11] 793-805.

[12] 806-807.

[13] 812-817, 822-857.

[14] 984-1015.

[15] 1016-1063. Avaritia nevertheless later makes use of this same measure (1068-1115).

[16] 1064-1067.

[17] 1116-1128, etc.

[18] 1187-1200. Hypocrisy speaks a stanza in this heavy measure also (1492-1498).

[19] 1244-1291.

[20] 1292-1326.

[21] 1327-1340.

down to five-stress couplets, in which even the change of act takes place. For Deus Pater *solus* the rime royal is reserved,[22] and his entourage is content with pentameter couplets. Toward the end of the play the redintegration of the Three Laws being accomplished, rime royal is bestowed upon Fides Christiana[23] and the protagonists as well.[24] This is the true end of the play, but the Bishop has appended a song and six lines of rimed tetrameter which condense the decalogue into a compass so small that one cannot help smiling.[25]

Rime royal is reserved for characters of dignity and, with a sole exception, good. As a rule, too, it serves to conclude if not always to begin the acts of the drama. Particularly at the beginning and end of the play it is employed to impress the audience with the beauty and good properties of the Three Laws as well as with the power and dignity of Balaeus and Deus Pater. Rime couée is used throughout Act II, in which Infidelitas works the destruction of Naturae Lex, and thereafter only returns with the chief vice sporadically. For the rest, couplets bear up the interlude and furnish the mortar by which these "Lapides Preciosi" are set into the tower of vituperation that the Bishop has erected against the "Sodomytes, Pharysees and Papystes."

[22] 1894-1921, 1954-1974.
[23] 1996-2002, 2075-2081.
[24] 2005-2074.
[25] 61-66 of the epilogue.

XXIX. God's Promises[1]

Text: E. E. Jones, ed. (Erlangen, 1909).
Date: 1538.[2]
Rhythm: heavy.
Prevailing metre: pentameter rime royal.

Lines:	952	%
Dissyllabic rime:	92	9.7
Trisyllabic rime:	2	.2
Redundant rime:	7	.7
Rime lacking:	1	.1
Latin rime:	2	.2
Unrimed Latin:	1	.1
Linkage:	47	4.9
Pentameter rime royal:	601	63.1
Pentameter couplets:	338	35.5
Pentameter leash:	13	1.4

The metre of *God's Promises* falls neatly into two groups, couplets and rime royal. The Chaucerian strophe, following custom, belongs to Balaeus Prolocutor in the prologue[3] and to Pater Coelestis at the beginning of Act I.[4] Adam veers to couplets,[5] but he returns to rime royal in his philosophy.[6] There are hereafter interloping couplets for the conversations with Adam,[7] but when Pater Coelestis speaks with authority, he uses rime royal.[8] For long speeches this stanza seems most congenial, for Adam,[9] Pater Coelestis,[10]

[1] Text, pp. xvi-xix; Brandl, p. lxi; Reyher, p. 59.

[2] Eckhardt, i. 5.

[3] 1-35. As Prolocutor, Bale also concludes the play in rime royal, 918-952.

[4] 36-77.

[5] 83-91.

[6] 92-98.

[7] 107-113.

[8] 114-134.

[9] 144-178.

[10] 36-77, 114-134, 179-199, 254-260, 293-313, 383-389, 539-545, 592-598, 626-639, 750-756, 778-791, 827-833, 836-842, 855-861, 872-878.

Justus, Noah,[11] Abraham Fidelis,[12] Moses Sanctus,[13] David Rex Pius,[14] Esaias Propheta,[15] and Johannes Baptista.[16] There is, however, nothing distinguishing in their use of this stanza form; they are all capable of speaking in couplets to each other.

The only common thread one can find to link together the stanzas of rime royal is that they are used to speak more to the audience than to the characters on-stage. Whatever John Bale wanted his parishioners (for so he must have considered all those who attended his interludes and listened to his diatribes on the Papists as if they were sermons) to mark and learn he put into the seven-line stanza;[17] otherwise couplets were adequate. He seems to have given more thought to making the verses stanzaic than to adapting them to anything within the play. The use of scheme is elementary and must be looked on as without great importance.

[11] 219-239, 267-273, 286-292.
[12] 395-415.
[13] 518-538.
[14] 546-566, 640-660.
[15] 675-689, 757-777.
[16] 792-826, 883-917.
[17] A ramification of this is to be seen in his method of concluding one act and beginning the next in rime royal.

XXX. John the Baptist[1]

Text: J. S. Farmer, ed., *The Dramatic Writings of John Bale* (London, 1907), pp. 129-150.
Date: 1538.[2]
Rhythm: light.
Prevailing metre: tetrameter couplets.

Lines:	488	%
Dissyllabic rime:	42	8.6
Redundant rime:	1	.2
Tetrameter couplets:	327	67.1
Tetrameter rime royal:	126	25.9
Pentameter rime royal:	35	7.2

"John Baptist's Preaching in the Wilderness" is in prosody very close to *God's Promises* in consisting of rime royal and couplets. Praefacio is given by Baleus Prolocutor again in rime royal[3]—in light fours for comparison; then "incipit comoedia" with Joannes Baptista.[4] Up to this point there is rime royal, but Turba Vulgaris and the Publican and Soldier he brings along with him speak in the dramatic doggerel. Rime royal returns in the confession of Turba Vulgaris at his conversion,[5] but in tumbling verse John the Baptist shrives him of his sins.[6] The same thing happens in the baptism and absolution of the other two infidels.[7] When Jesus Christus comes, speaking in the light rime royal which becomes gradually heavier,[8] baptism (but without absolution) follows in the light rimed tetrameter.[9] Jesus kneels and

[1] Brandl, p. lxi.
[2] Eckhardt, i. 5.
[3] 1-35.
[4] 36-49.
[5] 114-120.
[6] 121-138.
[7] Publicanus confesses in the light tetrameter rime royal (139-145) and is shriven by Joannes Baptista in tetrameter couplets (146-163); Miles Armatus confesses thus too (164-170) and is shriven (171-337).
[8] 338-372.
[9] 373-424.

thanks God,[10] and Pater Coelestis replies in the same rime royal.[11] At this, John the Baptist also kneels and sings his praises for what he has witnessed.[12] The drama comes to an end when Baleus Prolocutor has spoken his five stanzas of heavy rime royal.[13]

The simplicity of purpose in the riming that Bale made use of in this drama almost precludes any attempt to define it. There is only one act, and the interlude itself is but half-size. There are no boundaries to be traced in the schemes. The only thing one can say is that for the actual "business" of the play, couplets prove sufficient, but that when the element of divine contact enters, either in prayer or in the words of exhortation of Pater Coelestis, Jesus, or John the Baptist, rime royal is the measure employed. There is discrimination in the use of the metres, but it is not of striking import, and they cannot be charged with variety.

[10] 425-431.

[11] 432-445.

[12] 446-453 .in couplets. The doxology is actually sung or intoned (454-457).

[13] 458-492.

XXXI. The Temptation of Our Lord[1]

Text: J. S. Farmer, ed., *The Dramatic Writings of John Bale* (London, 1907), pp. 153-170.
Date: 1538.[2]
Rhythm: light.
Prevailing metre: tetrameter couplets.

Lines:	433	%
Dissyllabic rime:	38	8.8
Identical rime:	2	.5
Latin rime:	1	.2
Rime lacking:	1	.2
Tetrameter couplets:	321	74.0
Tetrameter rime royal:	112	25.9

What applies to the interludes of Bale previously noted applies also here. There are the thirty-five lines of preface or prologue, and the thirty-five lines of epilogue in light tetrameter rime royal, and between them is the trunk of the play in dramatic doggerel. From the structure of these interludes, by the way in which the rime royal is carried over from the prologue into the body of the play, it would appear that the author attempted to plan his work on the style of the *Three Laws*, with rime royal for the protagonists and couplets for the stars of lesser magnitude. The rapid demise of such a scheme points to the unwillingness of the dramatist to sustain his system, whether because of the poetical effort involved or not; at any rate, it has an odd look that denies facility, let alone felicity, to the versifier.

In this "brefe Comedy or enterlude" of the Temptation the same situation is renewed. Baleus Prolocutor speaks the Praefatio in the light tetrameter rime royal,[3] which carries over into the body of the play in the words of Jesus

[1] Brandl, p. lxi; Reyher, p. 59.
[2] Eckhardt, i. 6.
[3] 1-35.

Christus.[4] Satan Tentator speaks in this same measure in an encomium on himself.[5] The light tetrameter couplets arrive when Satan begins his attempts at beguilement,[6] and this is the vehicle for the rest of the interlude. With Satan expelled and the angels approaching, the tumbling verse abides until John Bale comes out to deliver the epilogue in five stately heptastichs.[7]

[4] 36-56.
[5] 57-77.
[6] 78-398.
[7] 399-433.

XXXII. King John[1]

Text: W. W. Greg and J. H. P. Pafford, ed., for the Malone Society (London, 1931).
Date: 1539.[2]
Rhythm: heavy.
Prevailing metre: pentameter couplets.

Lines:[3]	2678	%
Dissyllabic rime:	304	11.4
Trisyllabic rime:	10	.4
Redundant rime:	28	1.0
Identical rime:	6	.2
Latin rime:	17	.6
Greek rime:	1	..
Unrimed Latin:	21	.8
Rime lacking:	7	.3
Linkage:	2	.1
Pentameter couplets:[4]	2307	86.1
Pentameter rime royal:	325	12.2
Pentameter leash:	35	1.3
Pentameter quatrain:	12	.5

The long gangling lines of this last[2, 3] of Bale's works differ considerably from those of his others. They are here considered as tumid pentameters,[4] although Saintsbury's term "Alexandrine"[1] is often justifiable. It is a matter more of dodecasyllabics than of five or six stresses. And if the syllabication is careless, so is the riming: the same tags do over and over again. The patterns are two-fold: rime royal, and consecutive rime occasionally varied by alternation.

The king opens the interlude in heavy rime royal[5] which

[1] Brandl, p. lxi; Reyher, pp. 59-60; Saintsbury, i. 336-7.

[2] Text, p. xii (xi-xxiv); see also below, n. 3.

[3] Including, as do the rest of the figures, the marginal additions and the 175 lines on the additional page. Whiting (p. 99) considers the play as having 2645 lines and conjectures its date to have been 1536.

[4] Following the precedent of Brandl (above, n. 1).

[5] The manuscript is assumed to be in Bale's handwriting, and most of these stanzas of rime royal he noted in the margin by the Greek letter π. This π does not, however, belong exclusively to the rime royal, and one finds it setting off couplets as well (2343, 2349, 2363, etc.). Its paragraphic significance is not sustained.

changes, with the words of the widowed England,[6] to the loose pentameter couplets. For Sedition[7] as well as for Civil Order[8] the rimes alternate, and one cannot attach any importance to the interpolation of quatrains. Rime royal is restored after the deluge of couplets to conclude the first act, for Interpreter to "interpret" the events that have come to pass[9]—i.e. to moralize on the efforts of King John to reform the church, and his beguilement by Dissimulation. In Act II Sedition[10] addresses Nobility with his lies in rime royal, and King John[11] in majesty speaks of history in this measure. Later he nobly soliloquizes on the evil that popery has done to him and his state.[12] The eulogy Verity[13] pronounces on the king's departure is in the same metrical vein.[14] Imperial Majesty plucks allusion from the Bible in this style[15] and browbeats the villainous Sedition later.[16] In righteous indignation they conclude the piece in rime royal with slight interruptions from the staple couplets;[17] Nobility, Clergy, and Civil Order adorn the Bishop's tale by pointing the moral.[18]

As the long pentameter couplets sustain the greater part of the play, there is seen to be little method in the application of the rime royal. It serves to denote the key characters and to underscore certain reflective passages which mirror the action. It is used without discrimination of character, merely as a device to attract attention and to give to thoughtful

[6] 22-764.

[7] 765-768.

[8] 383-386.

[9] 1076-1110. This stately metre was not sacred from the depredations of Usurped Power (945-979) or Dissimulation (1002-1025).

[10] 1174-1180.

[11] 1277-1304.

[12] Text, p. 83, add. p. I, 115-128 = 2002-2015. Also 2112-2132.

[13] Like the character of this name in *A Satire of the Three Estates* (pp. 70-3); she does not use rime royal.

[14] 2145-2172.

[15] 2318-2338.

[16] 2548-2554.

[17] 2585-2603.

[18] 2604-2645.

words thoughtful form. In the canon of John Bale's dramatic work, it is a turning backward to easier methods of writing as well as a looking forward to the later days of the century when his quasi-Alexandrine would be cut irreparably down into the dramatic doggerel of four stresses.[19]

[19] A tabulation of Bale's metrics as disclosed in the five interludes has the following composition:

	Tetrameter couplets	Pentameter couplets	Tetrameter rime royal	Pentameter rime royal	Polysyllabic rime	Redundant rime
	%	%	%	%	%	%
Three Laws:	7.7	37.3	...	17.4	12.0	1.0
God's Promises:	...	36.9	...	63.1	9.9	.7
John the Baptist:	67.1	...	25.9	7.2	8.6	...
The Temptation:	73.9	...	25.9	...	8.8	...
King John:	...	87.4	...	12.2	11.8	1.0

The table is suggestive of chronology although all the plays but *King John* are dated 1538. The *Three Laws* contains a large amount of rime couée (27.3%) which does not appear above. This might indicate an earlier date of composition; or more certainly an earlier technic, for Bale had already begun to thunder against Rome from across the Irish Sea.

A characteristic of his versification is love of jingle and reiterated sound. This is made clear in the large quantities of feminine rime and in the way in which a couplet, though complete, might irresistibly urge another rime, to produce redundancy. These tendencies, more subjective than the other aspects of prosody, never forsook him. *King John,* which is usually thought to be later than the other dramas because of its profane subject and more maturely artistic grasp of the playwright's tools (see, however, p. 90, nn. 2, 3), is marked by the introduction, hesitating though it is, of the heroic stanza, and the very lines grow longer. The generally accepted chronology, then, is borne out by the internal evidence of the metrics.

XXXIII. (The History of) Jacob and Esau[1]

Text: J. S. Farmer, ed., *Six Anonymous Plays* (London, 1906), ii. 2-90.
Date: 1545.[2]
Rhythm: light.
Prevailing metre: tetrameter couplets.

Lines:	1702	%
Dissyllabic rime:	136	8.0
Trisyllabic rime:	7	.4
Identical rime:	10	.6
Rime lacking:	28	1.6
Tetrameter couplets:	1643	97.1
Tetrameter rime royal:	49	2.9

Simplicity is the keystone of the prosody of *Jacob and Esau.* But for the prologue and epilogue, the whole play is in the dramatic doggerel, which carries on without a break from scene to scene and act to act. The introductory matter is presented in rime royal, and the Poet speaks the peroration in this same traditional strophe. The least variation occurs in the prayer of Isaac and Rebecca in tetrameter couplets when the epilogue is complete, and on this the interlude reaches its termination. The author of *Jacob and Esau,* whether or not he was Nicholas Udall,[3] had small concern for his prosody. He rimed well,[4] wrote his introduction and conclusion in the traditional rime royal, and the drama in dramatic metre. His was a wholly practical approach to prosody, and the intransigence of his tumbling verse makes manifest the solidity of his attitude.

[1] Bradner, pp. 379-80; Brandl, p. lxi; Saintsbury, i. 341; Schipper, i. 255-6.

[2] Whiting, p. 48.

[3] See p. 52, n. 8, for a summary of Heywood's metrical characteristics: from internal evidence one might deduce him to be the author of *Jacob and Esau.* For the thesis that Udall wrote it, see C. W. Wallace, *The Evolution of the English Drama up to Shakespeare* (Berlin, 1912), p. 101. Bradner (above, n. 1) has shown its syllable count to be the percentile equivalent of *Roister Doister's.*

[4] "Jacob" and "Esau" provide the only interesting rimes in the play. The former is rimed with the meaningless "kakob" (II. iii. 29/30), and the latter is for a long time not rimed at all. At times it goes with Ragan (I. i. 50/1, 88/9, 116/7), you (V. i. 1/2; ii. 1/2), and thou (V. vi. 21/2, 36/7).

XXXIV. THE NICE WANTON[1]

Text: Manly, i. 457-480.
Date: 1547.[2]
Rhythm: light.
Prevailing metre: tetrameter couplets.

Lines:[3]	528	%
Dissyllabic rime:	16	3.1
Trisyllabic rime:	2	.4
Redundant rime:	7	1.3
Latin rime:	1	.2
Rime lacking:	12	2.3
Tetrameter couplets:	218	39.4
Tetrameter rime royal:	102	19.3
Tetrameter quatrain:	92	17.4
Tetrameter ballad-six:	24	4.6
Common measure:	8	1.5
Pentameter rime royal:	7	1.3
Dimeter quatrain:	4	.8
Miscellaneous:[4]	73	13.8

The Nice Wanton has a profusion of measures, not all of them legitimate. The prologue begins the drama in anapæstic quatrains of four stresses,[5] and Barnabas continues in this vein,[6] the only difference being that his verse is less jaunty, in keeping with his character. Ismael[7] and Dalila come in singing gracelessly, and the three engage in conversation in the dramatic doggerel.[8] Dalila employs a long measure,[9] Ismael a common measure,[10] and a second song proves pre-

[1] Saintsbury, i. 341.

[2] Eckhardt, i. 50.

[3] Exclusive of the two quatrains, one in trimeter and the other in tetrameter, prefixed to the interlude.

[4] Including the trimeter riming abacbx (71-76), the tetrameter quasi-leash abaaa (177-181), fragments like the axa of 258-260, and the string of tetrameter ababacccccc (374-384).

[5] 1-24.

[6] 25-36.

[7] See p. 82, n. 10.

[8] 37-38, 41-62.

[9] 63-66.

[10] 67-70.

lude to the tetrametric rime royal of Eulalia,[11] with whom the mother Xantippe holds parley in couplets[12] and a ballad-six of indefinite linear dimensions.[13] Iniquity speaks in dimeter quatrain,[14] and he with the wantons plays at dice in the doggerel tetrapodies.[15] Again song intervenes.[16] The play is carried forward in couplets; but when Dalila goes out as young and returns haggard and wretched, the lapse of time is accented by the employment of alternate rime, in which she makes her moan.[17] Barnabas chides his sister in rime royal[18] as if he were judge Daniel, who also uses the seven-line measure.[19] When all speak together, couplets suffice,[20] as they do for the grafting "Baily,"[21] and theirs is the agency that conveys the verdict of the trial. Worldly Shame comes to point his scorn in hexastichs,[22] and Xantippe's remonstrances continue in couplcts.[23] Worldly Shame in common measure vilipends the shrew,[24] who in alternate rime would slay herself.[25] The good Barnabas is at hand with rime royal and words of censure for his mother.[26] There are also words of good counsel for the audience in this pattern,[27] and the interlude is brought down to the "Finis" with a prayer for the Queen in the long pentameter Chaucerian strophe.[28]

In perspective, the prosody of *The Nice Wanton* is a

[11] 82-106.
[12] 122-134.
[13] 135-140.
[14] 146-149.
[15] 150-193.
[16] 194-205.
[17] 261-284.
[18] 285-291.
[19] 343-349, 385-391.
[20] 392-458.
[21] 350-373.
[22] 459-470.
[23] 471-472.
[24] 473-476.
[25] 477-488.
[26] 489-523.
[27] 524-544.
[28] 545-552.

reversion to the pre-Heywood type of interlude, like those also included by Manly. There is, however, a certain amount of method in the assigning of rime royal to such characters as the well-meaning Eulalia and Barnabas,[29] the use of couplets for the more vicious scenes, and that of quatrains for those in which good strives with ill, however ineffectively. The three stages of good are thus set above one another in accord with the procedure so long ago established by Medwall, but with little more attention to such detail than the author of *Hickscorner* or *The World and the Child* gave it. The advance of time in this type of interlude is seen in the epiphany of rime royal, but it is with these earlier plays that it deserves comparison as its prosody, although in their tradition, makes a great stride forward.

[29] We must consider them as exponents of the good element in *The Nice Wanton* without otherwise judging them. As a personality, Eulalia is almost as bad as the poisonous little Barnabas.

XXXV. John Bon and Mast Parson

Text: W. H. Black, ed., for the Percy Society (London, 1851), xxx.
Date: 1548.[1]
Rhythm: light.
Alliteration: occasional.
Prevailing metre: tetrameter couplets.

Lines:	172	%
Dissyllabic rime:	20	11.5
Trisyllabic rime:	2	1.2
Redundant rime:	7	4.1
Latin rime:	2	1.2
Tetrameter couplets:	165	95.9
Tetrameter rime royal:	7	4.1

The body of this play is wholly in the rimed tetrameter, and prosodically it deserves little comment. The one stave of rime royal, likewise light, is given to the prologue.

The only distinction one can note is that the tetrameters grow heavier during the periods of altercation, of literal storm and stress.[2] Later on, the Parson also uses the heavier line,[3] but there is no particular reason for it. If a trend is to be observed in the versification, it is in the gradual increase in the number of syllables to the line as the interlude proceeds; but the author, Luke Shepherd, cannot be said to have altered his prosody with any motive in view.

[1] Text, pp. v-vii.
[2] 57-61, 84-90.
[3] 132-133.

XXXVI. Impatient Poverty[1]

Text: R. B. McKerrow, ed., *Materialen zur Kunde des älteren englischen Dramas* (Louvain, 1911), xxxiii.
Date: 1550.[2]
Rhythm: light.
Prevailing metre: tetrameter couplets.

Lines:	1097	%
Dissyllabic rime:	24	2.2
Latin rime:	4	.4
French rime:	2	.2
(A. Miscellaneous couplets:	569	51.8
B. Miscellaneous rime couée:	253	23.1)
Tetrameter couplets:	430	39.2
Tetrameter triplets:	153	13.9
Pentameter rime royal:	101	9.2
Tetrameter sixain coué:	78	7.1
Tetrameter octave couée:	64	5.8
Tetrameter rime royal:	35	3.2
Tetrameter quatrain:	8	.7
Pentameter quatrain:	4	.4
Miscellaneous:[3]	224	20.4

It does not seem possible to reduce the prosody of *Impatient Poverty* to a very scientific basis. It is an odyssey of bad verse: the lines are of an indeterminate length, they rime by twos or threes at random, and there is little method in the way in which they are strung together. Whenever one meets a rime couée in a morass of couplets and tercets, or encounters a ballad stave among verses that rime with licence, one feels that the author has stumbled into it by coincidence and error, and that he is soon to be mending his ways, riming

[1] Text, p. xiii.

[2] Text, p. x.

[3] No order can be brought to these lines. Occasional abba rimes are to be discovered, but the beats do not submit to counting (509-512, 724-727, 840-843, etc.).

by accident as before. This can be illustrated by the catalogue:

Like all good interludes, it begins and ends with rime royal; Peace provides the prologue[4] and epilogue.[5] Envy, the vice, argues with Peace in rimed doggerel[6] which Peace interrupts with rime royal.[7] Rime couée marks the dialogue following of Impatient Poverty and the ameliorating force.[8] Conscience breaks in with a Chaucerian stanza[9] which yields to schemes that defy analysis.[10] Peace later makes a few comments in rime royal whose verses observe no norm,[11] a privilege shared with Power[12] and Abundance.[13] Four stanzas of it conclude the play.[14]

In spite, then, of the prosodic mess which this work is, it appears that the playwright noticed his versification, although he handled it in the crudest fashion. Peace, presiding angel, prologue and epilogue, is allowed to use the dignified measure, and the rest of the characters are condemned to occasionally alternate and successive rime. The scenes of vice near the beginning of the play are thought most worthy of tail-rime, but the writer's purpose soon yields to the facile welter that follows. The only relic of his former desire to preserve a prosodic difference and balance is to be found in the treatment of Peace as the play moves to its end. The three vague groups of rime royal, rime couée, and couplets (replete, it must be added, with leakage) maintain their

[4] 1-22.

[5] 1084-1097.

[6] 23-94.

[7] 95-102.

[8] Following 137. It occurs at intervals to 404, broken by insignificant rime royal (201-215).

[9] 405-411; see p. 51, n. 3.

[10] 412-792 contain straggling rimes couées whose appearance is fitful (441-448, 485-493, 517-522, 728-734). After this, indeed after the first third of the drama, it is sparingly sprinkled among the couplets, etc., which follow (896-902).

[11] 793-812.

[12] 721-934, 994-1000.

[13] 946-952.

[14] 1070-1097. From the third of these stanzas the fifth line is missing.

identity through the first third of it. Thereafter there is but a frail awareness of the play-writer that he has a well defined measure like rime royal left in his verse-bag, and this he withdraws at the last moment as if to persuade the audience that his metrical variation had been going on all the while. No one can question that the verse slips easier along without the gyves of elaborate stanzaic exigences of rime; yet the result cannot be scrutinized prosodically. It is enough to say that the ends of the play were rounded with a little rime royal after the correct models of Heywood and his peers.

XXXVII. Lusty Juventus[1]

Text: J. S. Farmer, ed., *The Dramatic Works of R. Wever and Thomas Ingelend* (London, 1905), pp. 1-42.
Date: 1550.[2]
Rhythm: light.
Prevailing metre: tetrameter rime royal.

Lines:	1234	%
Dissyllabic rime:	69	5.6
Redundant rime:	21	1.7
Identical rime:	7	.6
Internal rime:	11	.9
Rime lacking:	33	2.7
Linkage:	29	2.4
Tetrameter rime royal:	582	47.1
Tetrameter couplets:	218	17.7
Tetrameter sixain coué:	70	5.7
Trimeter, abba:	24	1.9
Tetrameter octave couée:	18	1.5
Tetrameter quatrain:	16	1.3
Pentameter rime royal:	14	1.1
Heptameter couplets:	13	1.1
Tetrameter ballad-eight:	8	.6
Dimeter, abba:	4	.3
Miscellaneous:[3]	279	22.1

The only work by which R. Wever can be judged is, in the words of Saintsbury,[1] "partly in the short, partly in the long [doggerel]." The short lines, however, constitute about a fiftieth of the play; but the lines are by no means regular,[4] no more regular than the riming. Half a sixain coué

[1] Saintsbury, i. 341.

[2] Whiting, p. 107.

[3] The size of this category betrays hit-or-miss poetics. It is futile to attempt to order the batches or rime sprinkled throughout in 110-126, 319-324, 482-491, 634-686, etc. The most flagrant case is to be found before the second song, in 969-979, in the tetrameter which rimes xxxaaaxbbcc. The *x*'s are independent of rime.

[4] Varying from two beats (387, 390, 630-633, etc.) to seven (1235-1247).

is left straggling on time and again,[5] and the rimes are on occasion monstrous.[6] From the prosodic point of view this drama is an *olla podrida* of slipshod versifying.

Berdan[7] has taken the printer of this work, John Awdely, to task for having upset the text of the songs with extra syllables, contending that they were written in the syllabic tradition of the mediæval Latinists.[8] The double refrains in the songs do suggest one of the stricter Latin forms, but beyond that it is hardly safe to go. If the syllabic theories of John Garland were fast ensconced in the mind of Wever, it does not seem likely that he would have perpetrated the prosodic *galimatias* that is *Lusty Juventus*. On the contrary, he would have inclined to do as Udall, the schoolmaster and diligent student of Latin, was to do:[9] he would have rejoiced in syllabic constraint as an artistic stimulus like a true classicist, and he would not have been moved to return to the lazy ways of writing into which this interlude has fallen. Prosodically considered, it is one of the worst, a fair counterpart to *Damon and Pythias* with its rimed prose. The setter of type would have had to spend his nights waking in order to convert a regularly versified drama, stricter by far in style than *Gorboduc* with its inexorable blank verse, into the present salmagundi. No; it is most likely that Wever, like Awdely,[10] was innocent of the poetic treatises that so affected French poetry.[11] Wever was most probably not in the least interested in the mechanics, syllabic or otherwise, of what he was writing. He was too busy, like John Bale, with the Papists to have time either for mediæval Latin poetics or for English poetics. He took up

[5] 76-78, 89-91, etc.

[6] Desire/clear (280/1), say / may / lie (835/7/8), nonce / bones / acquaintance (833/4/6), show/due (1167/8; an ocular rime).

[7] Op. cit., pp. 152-3.

[8] See pp. 3-4, 193.

[9] *Roister Doister* admits no lines of less than eleven syllables or more than thirteen. Even the thirteeners are proportionately rare (6%); see Bradner, p. 378.

[10] See A. L. Reade, "John 'Awdelay,' the Printer," *Times Literary Supplement* (1932), xxxi. 331.

[11] See pp. 193-4.

rime royal and rime couée because they were at hand, and he maltreated them in his own particular way because he was not interested in treating them well.

The abandon with which the lines are constructed is equalled by that with which they are assigned to characters. Rime royal is given to the Messenger as Prologue,[12] to Juventus especially,[13] to the Devil,[14] to Hypocrisy,[15] to Abominable Living,[16] and to Good Counsel.[17] Anyone of consequence speaks in this measure as if to command the attention and respect of the audience by so cadencing his verses. God's Promises,[18] borrowed from Bishop Bale, speaks by nature in this style. Good or bad, there is no discrimination; it is but Wever's method of italicizing a scene. Hypocrisy, however, is not consistently worthy of the rime royal and is for the most part relegated to rime couée because he is a lesser evil.[19] He also makes use of an extraordinary stanza like the ballad-six with the third and fourth rimes reversed before settling into his tail-rime.[20] Satan's use of rime royal is impressive in one particular place:[21] as he becomes more and more emotionally aroused, his lines become longer and lighter. For filler, couplets are useful. When the play comes to its end under the hegemony of Good Counsel and the reformed Juventus, it is in rime royal as would be expected, but topped off with an extra tercet.[22]

To sum up, the manner in which R. Wever handled rime is three-fold: for the scenes which he wished to impress upon the audience and for characters of particular importance he chose rime royal, for the spineless Hypocrisy he had rime couée of long and short kinds, and to mortar the inter-

[12] 1-36.

[13] 79-88, 103-109, 156-169, 249-269, 756-762, etc.

[14] 445-458, etc.

[15] 475-481, 694-714.

[16] 892-898, 962-968.

[17] 998-1032, 1072-1106, 1248-1254.

[18] 1164-1234; see pp. 84-5.

[19] 763-769, 875-880, 908-913.

[20] 387-398.

[21] 325-359.

[22] 1255-1264.

stices of his drama he had couplets. This is not a manner that is worked out with fineness, for Wever gave little thought to his versification. He devoted himself to extolling Protestantism at its expense, and when he was able to point his morals by putting them into one particular kind of rime scheme, it came as grist to his indignant mill. The other considerations are secondary, and the use of the metres is due to his desire for making his points and the better to fix the attention of an audience.

XXXVIII. Mary Magdalene[1]

Text: F. I. Carpenter, ed., *The Life and Repentance of Marie Magdalene* (Chicago, 1904).
Date: 1550.[2]
Rhythm: light.
Prevailing metre: tetrameter quatrain.

Lines:	2116	%
Dissyllabic rime:	305	14.4
Trisyllabic rime:	4	.2
Identical rime:	2	.1
Latin rime:	2	.1
Greek rime:	1	..
Rime lacking:	5	.2
Unrimed Latin:[3]	8	.4
Tetrameter quatrain:	1328	62.7
Tetrameter couplets:	586	27.7
Pentameter couplets:[3]	90	4.3
Pentameter rime royal:	84	4.0
Pentameter quatrain:	24	1.1
Tetrameter leash:	4	.2

The long prologue of *Mary Magdalene* is in the pentameter rime royal,[4] which thereafter vanishes from the morality. In what is comparatively good anapæstic verse Mary, led by Infidelity, enters and succumbs to his blandishments in quatrains;[5] and when she departs, the verse changes to the less anapæstic but consistently light rimed tetrameter.[6] This is due to the coming of the other vices, Pride, Cupidity, and others, who teach her all kinds of sin, even employing song to that end.[7] Mary is an apt pupil, and the *scæna* is cleared

[1] Text, pp. xxi-xxiv; Ramsay, pp. cxlii-cxliii.

[2] Text, p. xv.

[3] From the summary are excluded two Latin elegiac couplets (707-710) and one dactylic hexameter (121).

[4] 1-86 on pp. 3-5.

[5] 1-234.

[6] 235-842.

[7] 783-802.

to permit Simon the Pharisee and Malicious Judgment to speak in alternate rime of Jesus and of matters theological and controversial in order to expound the thesis of the "learned clarke Lewis Wager," who was caught in the toils of this strife.[8] Christ effects a brief alteration in prayer[9] using the iambic pentameter quatrain; but when that is concluded, the light cross-rime returns.[10] This prevails until the end is in sight, when Mary enters with Justification, all the vices being gone. They and Love bring the interlude to its finish in heavy pentameter couplets, speaking of the religion and the moral which the audience were to carry home with them.[11]

There was thus reason in the employment of the various measures by the playwright. In following tradition he used rime royal for his prologue and dramatic doggerel for scenes at the beginning of his drama in which the vices frolicked; but he departed from the old ways in making use of alternate rime for the bulk of his work. The whole drama, with its controversial sophistication, belongs to this metre, which becomes artistically varied in the prayer to the more majestic heroic stanzas. To provide a reflective summary of the things he wished to convey, Lewis Wager appended a kind of moral epilogue in heroic couplets, once again drawing attention to his change of matter in the manner of presentation. He is shown to have been very solicitous of the different styles of versification, aware of the effect to be wrought by changing them according to what he was demonstrating on-stage for the anti-interdenominationalistically inclined, and manipulating them with a dexterity remarkable in the Tudor interlude of the middle period.

[8] 843-1454.

[9] 1455-1478.

[10] 1479-1962.

[11] 1963-2052.

XXXIX. Somebody, Avarice, and Minister[1]

Text: W. W. Greg, ed., for the Malone Society, "Collections" (London, 1931), II. iii. 253-256.
Date: 1550.[2]
Rhythm: light.
Prevailing metre: tetrameter couplets.

Lines:	140	%
Tetrameter couplets:	140	100.

This little dramatic fragment is written exclusively in dramatic doggerel, the rimed tetrameter, and provides no matter for prosodic comment. Dated about 1550 by the editor, it provides, if anything, only an additional straw in the wind, attesting the popularity of this easily written measure. Somebody, Avarice, and Minister "spoyle Veryte" in a "vice scene" that moves in tumbling verse. It, like the Reford fragments, is presented here solely to make the canon of interludes as complete as possible.

[1] Brandl, p. lxi.
[2] Eckhardt, i. 29.

XL. Tom Tyler and His Wife[1]

Text: F. E. Schelling, ed., *Publications of the Modern Language Association* (1900), xv. 261-287.
Date: 1550.[2]
Rhythm: light.
Prevailing metre: dimeter couplets.

Lines:	729	%
Dissyllabic rime:	218	29.9
Trisyllabic rime:	2	.3
Redundant rime:	12	1.6
Identical rime:	1	.1
Internal rime:	21	2.9
Dimeter couplets:[3]	380	52.1
Tetrameter couplets:	122	16.7
Trimeter couplets:	65	8.9
Trimeter couplets:[4]	28	3.8
Octameter couplets:	4	.5
Miscellaneous:[5]	130	17.8

[1] Text, p. 256.

[2] Whiting, p. 189.

[3] Printed somewhat like the rime couée of *Godly Queen Hester* (p. 48, nn. 3, 4), the wheel in one line and the tail in the next. Our text is that of the "second impression," 1661, when the comedy was a hundred years old; the printer has quite obscured the prosodic lineaments of his piece. Single dimeter couplets are interspersed with the arrangement noted above (103-137). When the rime becomes misplaced, the verse is allowed to stagger on until it rights itself (345-363, 718-728). To show the schemes of versification as the author planned them, nothing short of rewriting the entire interlude will suffice. A stichic and hemistichic catalogue of the rimes (see below, n. 5) throws no further light on the prosody of this work, and the great miscellany which embraces them only bears out the principle of tagging alternate stresses with rime.

[4] Printed as hemistichs, with internal rime.

[5] In general, there are two rimes and four beats to each line, creating a prosody of hemistichs. If a space be used to designate the end of a line, the rimes in 196-200 (for instance) can be denoted as follows: a a b bc cd de ef fg g h hi ij xj, etc. This kind of thing can be duplicated *ad libitum*; these passages are exemplary: 300-370, 385-440, 676-841 (the end), with occasional interruptions from rimed trimeter and

The work of Francis Kirkman, who printed *Tom Tyler,* has converted into internal rime what are in truth nothing but the familiar couplets, which bear the rule far and away in this interlude. For a general summary, the words of Scott[6] are quite accurate: " 'In the doggerel style, the inner rime, the deadly iteration of jingle, the occasional forced rimes, and other details, the play accords with similar features more or less present in other pieces of the middle third of the sixteenth century.' "

The prologue is in the twenty riming lines of five heavy feet, which forthwith give way to those of two. Succeeding them in irregular jingle come lines with internal rime to create a hopeless conglomeration. Desire and Destiny boil the dramatic pot in the most irregular of rimed dimeter in order to make things ready for the entrance of the hapless Tom Tyler. Tom enters singing: the whole interlude, so small in compass, is constructed around the seven songs, and what prosody there is (and what drama there is) waits on the lyric doorstep. The ideal of versification appears to be rime's tagging every alternate beat,[7] producing a series of hemistichs that fills in the space between the songs. The bibulous activity of Strife and her gossips takes place in this style, and the final moralizing lesson conveyed in the chastening of both Tom Taylor and Tom Tyler. The riming lines of four stresses that appear at intervals are without significance, only for a sign that the playwright is relaxing the rigid discipline of Skeltonic doggerel. The rimed tetrameter is chiefly belonging to the wails of the assaulted Strife,[8] Tom Tyler's spouse, whom Tom Taylor has just beaten. The exceptional amount of pate-breaking that goes forward in this interlude

tetrameter. Other devices herein contained are the hemistich quatrains (153-154) and occasional trimeter rimed hemistichically, ab b cc d d x x ee ff gg gh h i i jj kk l l mm nn o o pp q q rr s xt (489-516).

[6] Text, p. 256. He goes on to cite as examples *The Four P's* and *King John*; to them one might better add *Godly Queen Hester.*

[7] Two lines illustrative of the way in which metre can be warped are 362 and 363. The first consists of two amphibrachs, the second of a third pæon and an amphibrach.

[8] 486-516.

would find it more difficult to bear up under the more dignified longer doggerel, perhaps; certainly it provides fitting punctuation for the short doggerel in which the play is entirely written. The best word that can be applied to the prosody in trying to describe it from any angle whatever is "bad," monotonously and unrelievedly bad, of a uniform badness whose only merit is in its consistent keeping with the badness of the drama whose vehicle it is.

XLI. The Old Man and his Wife

Text: D. Laing, ed., *The Poetical Works of Sir David Lyndsay* (Edinburgh, 1879. 3 vols.), ii. 327-340.
Date: 1552.[1]
Rhythm: heavy.
Alliteration: marked.
Prevailing metre: tetrameter couplets.

Lines:	277	%
Dissyllabic rime:	12	4.3
Internal rime:	1	.4
Tetrameter couplets:	100	36.1
Pentameter couplets:	96	34.7
Trimeter sixain coué:	57	20.6
Pentameter ballad-eight:	24	8.7

Prefixed to the *Satire of the Three Estates* on the occasion of its presentation in 1552 was a preliminary interlude, *The Auld Man and his Wife*, a kind of proclamation heralding the *opus magnum*.[2] Prosodically it is Lindsay's great work writ small, for it is apparelled in the three types of measure here encountered in these plays: the couplet, the ballad stave, and tail-rime. The rhythm is heavy also and the alliteration similarly apparent. If one were required to submit proof that this induction were from the same hand as the *Satire of the Three Estates*, the evidence afforded by the facts of versification would be satisfactory.

Nuntius proclaims the coming play for 7 June 1552 in three staves of ballad-eight,[3] and the Cotter, having drunk his dram, is eager to be in attendance, speaking in rime couée.[4] Findlaw of the foot-band finds this the proper vehicle for his thick dialect and belligerent tactics.[5] Couplets sustain the rest of the episode.[6] The attitude of Sir David Lindsay has not altered, nor his use of the divers schemes of metre altered from the previous pattern of the long play here intended to follow.

[1] Text, p. 363.
[2] Which contains another interlude; see p. 72.
[3] 1-24.
[4] 25-48.
[5] 101-133.
[6] 49-100, 134-277.

XLII. Respublica[1]

Text: Brandl, pp. 283-358.
Date: 1553.[2]
Rhythm: light.
Alliteration: occasional.
Prevailing metre: tetrameter couplets.

Lines:	936	%
Dissyllabic rime:	36	3.9
Trisyllabic rime:	6	.6
Identical rime:	2	.2
Latin rime:	4	.4
Rime lacking:	1	.1
Tetrameter couplets:	825	88.2
Pentameter couplets:	58	6.2
Tetrameter quatrain:	40	4.3
Tetrameter leash:	13	1.4

Respublica is not complex seen from the standpoint of versification. The details of the verse have been carefully noted,[3] and there remains only to note the occasion for the use of the rarer forms. The first scene of the fifth act is written in the light tetrameter[4] quatrains; it is the monody of Misericordia, good genius of the piece, pointing the way to the felicitous end, an essay on compassion caused by the rehabilitation of Respublica. The couplets of five beats all occur in the prologue, long lines of introduction to the play which follows. And follow it does, in the tumbling verse through five acts, interrupted only by the forty lines of Misericordia's rumination.

[1] Bradner, pp. 379-80; Brandl, pp. lx-lxii; L. A. Magnus, ed. (London, 1905), pp. xxxi-xxxii.
[2] Whiting, p. 110.
[3] By Brandl and Magnus, above, n. 1.
[4] Here is no wish to quarrel with the word of Magnus that the play is in Alexandrines, and that the scheme is syllabic and not accentual. His work and that of Bradner would seem to controvert this assumption.

Whoever he was, the author of this drama took no interest in its prosodic structure. He was content to let it ramble along once it had got started. Only the words of Misericordia in philosophico-political prelude to the closing act are distinguished from the body of the play—for natural reasons in this controversial interlude, and the device they use is merely that of riming the alternate lines instead of the consecutive ones. Whether or not Udall wrote *Respublica*[5]—and the verse structure with its variants makes him somewhat more eligible than the others—it is plain that he did not have his eye on the metrics of what he was writing.

[5] This conclusion of Magnus is borne out by the syllable-counting of Bradner; see above, n. 1, p. 93; p. 125, n. 3.

XLIII. The Longer Thou Livest, the More Fool Thou Art

Text: A. Brandl, ed., *Shakespeare Jahrbuch* (1900), xxxvi. 16-64.
Date: 1559.[1]
Rhythm: light.
Prevailing metre: tetrameter quatrain.

Lines:	1948	%
Dissyllabic rime:	204	10.5
Trisyllabic rime:	6	.3
Latin rime:	9	.5
Unrimed Latin:	10	.5
Rime lacking:	4	.2
Repeated lines:[2]	14	.7
Prose:[4]	3	.2
Tetrameter quatrain:[3]	1868	96.0
Pentameter rime royal:	77	3.9

The prologue to this interlude of "W. Wager" is in the heavy pentameter rime royal. The introduction accomplished, Moros the hero makes his appearance singing, and it is soon seen that the drama is to take place in quatrains, each line generally of four beats. So it continues to the end, bumping occasionally over unorthodox rime when Discipline, in the last seven lines, begs for the actors and spectators the spiritual assistance that effected the decline and fall of Moros. The play ends as it began, in wretched rime royal.

The dramatist shows a discrimination of the two forms he employed, but he does not go beyond that as he does in his later work, *Enough is as Good as a Feast*. There are in this case two metrical groups, one for the drama and one for the moral commentary which precedes and follows. The sole

[1] Text, p. 2.
[2] Moros echoes the preceding line, 339-366.
[3] Beginning in trimeter, it gradually works up to the light tetrameter.
[4] The interruptions of Moros, brief as they are, are best considered as prose (488, 489, 491).

point of interest is that rime royal was still considered the stately measure, fit for philosophy (such as it is), and the quatrain less suited to the loftier portions of the work, probably because it was easier to write. The quatrain, too, is almost Wager's particular property, judging by the extent to which it is used in his work, a striking contrast to the usual couplets and rimes couées.

XLIV. The Conflict of Conscience[1]

Text: J. P. Collier, ed., *Five Old Plays* (London, 1851), pp. 5-78.
Date: 1560.[2]
Rhythm: light.
Alliteration: moderate.[3]
Prevailing metre: tetrameter rime royal.

Lines:	2133	%
Dissyllabic rime:	150	7.0
Trisyllabic rime:	2	.1
Redundant rime:	7	.3
Identical rime:	3	.1
Latin rime:	5	.2
Rime lacking:	2	.1
Tetrameter rime royal:	876	41.2
Heptameter rime royal:	845	39.6
Pentameter rime royal:	203	9.5
Tetrameter couplets:	104	4.9
Pentameter couplets:	6	.3
Miscellaneous:[4]	99	4.6

Nathaniel Woodes' interlude is mostly in rime royal of varying length.[5] The prologue begins with lines of five

[1] Saintsbury, i. 342; C. Wine, "Nathaniel Wood's 'Conflict of Conscience,'" *Publications of the Modern Language Association* (1935), 1. 662.

[2] Eckhardt, i. 30.

[3] Particularly noticeable about line 345.

[4] With the varied tetrameter ababccc (624-630), abbabcc (1000-1006), ababbb (1138-1143), and the lines of seven beats riming ababbcdcd (1487-1495), and abacbcc (2014-2020). Frequently in the case of the tetrameter the a-rimes have five stresses and the b-rimes four. This miscellany ought obviously to be added to the groups of rime royal above.

[5] There are two main sizes: the short kind whose lines are in the light tetrameter and contain about eleven syllables, and the long kind whose lines are in the heavy heptameters which contain about fourteen syllables. In between are the lines with five stresses (1035-1048, 1056-1062, 1115-1135, 1143-1149) and those of no mean length (1249-1255 have 5464455, 204-212 have 556565566, and 268-274 have 5556665).

beats and gradually, at the end, the lines have become extended to septenaries. Like *Paradise Lost*, this interlude begins with Satan: "High time it is for me to stir about," and he stirs about in rime royal that likewise shows this tendency to bulge.[6] The same situation obtains between Mathetes and Philologus in the second scene.[7] The sevens become thoroughly apparent in the didascalic material of Philologus.[8] At the outset, the second act begins in the pentameter Chaucerian strophe,[9] but it dwindles to its end through tetrameter.[10] It is devoted to Hypocrisy, Tyranny, and Avarice. Act III is begun by Philologus in the long heptastichs;[11] the second scene of three staves belongs to Hypocrisy.[12] In his iniquity he is assisted by Tyranny and Avarice as before, and they proceed in four-beat verse.[13] Caconos reverts to the heavy septenaries in soliloquy,[14] but when he converses with the vices, tumbling verse appears on the boards for the first time.[15] Hypocrisy unsuccessfully essays a rime royal to cap the third act,[16] and Act IV begins with stichomythic heroic couplets,[17] which the Cardinal and Hypocrisy alter to the light rime royal.[18] Scenes i-iv continue in the shorter—four- to five-beat—rime royal with eleven syllables to the line, with Philologus joining the vices.[19] The words of Suggestion precipitate the final deluge of long

It is necessary to count the syllables in every line. With septenaries, however, Woodes has settled his prosody so that he cannot be accused like Edwards (p. 133) of tagging prose with rime.

[6] 71-182. At 169 the extra beats become noticeable.

[7] 183-324.

[8] 268-295, etc.

[9] 324-330.

[10] 331-749.

[11] 751-786.

[12] 787-799, 800-806; his first two stanzas are long, the third short.

[13] 808-869.

[14] 871-904.

[15] 905-1000.

[16] 1001-1007. The rimes in the third and fourth lines are inverted; see above, n. 4.

[17] 1008-1013.

[18] 1014-1020, 1029-1035.

[19] 1036-1486.

rimes royal, i.e. of iambic septenaries, and in them occurs the *dénoûment* of what was scarcely a *nœud.*[20]

Of the two kinds of Chaucerian strophe that fuse without critical demarcation into each other, the purpose in their construction seems to be that for the scenes of evil characters, the short type was used, and for the scenes in which the good characters appear, the long kind was requisite. The brief passage of couplets belongs only to the farcical element which follows in the train of Caconos and his thick accent. The demarcation in this case too is neither hard nor fast; Philologus speaks in the short stanza as well as in the long one.[21] In general, however, the playwright appears to have intended the long lines for the conveying of dignity and virtue, and the shorter verses for vehicles of vicious force.

[20] 1487-2133. It also becomes expanded in conversation to ababbcdcd (1487-1495) and altered by Theologus to abacbcc (2014-2020), as in n. 4 above.

[21] IV. i-iv.

XLV. THE DISOBEDIENT CHILD[1]

Text: J. S. Farmer, ed., *The Dramatic Writings of R. Wever and Thomas Ingelend* (London, 1905), pp. 43-91.
Date: 1560.[2]
Rhythm: light.
Prevailing metre: tetrameter quatrains.

Lines:	1455	%
Dissyllabic rime:	60	4.1
Redundant rime:	1	.1
Identical rime:	3	.2
Latin rime:	1	.1
Rime lacking:	10	.7
Tetrameter quatrains:	933	64.1
Tetrameter couplets:[3]	376	25.8
Tetrameter ballad-six:	132	9.1
Leash:	12	.8

The Disobedient Child is written in simple schemes, the rime being at times immediate and at others alternate. The ballad measure of six lines catalogued above was scarcely conceived as a measure by itself, and most of the time it appears to have arisen fortuitously from mere juxtaposition of couplets to quatrains. The long light line of four beats is consistently maintained and endures no variation other than that indigenous to the doggerel of this nature, dramatic doggerel. The rimes are fair, the equal of those elsewhere encountered, and undistinguished.[4]

There is no apparent reason for the use at one time of the quatrain and at another of the couplet. From the very beginning they are flung together at random,[5] and the irrational variation from one to the other is devoid of significance

[1] Saintsbury, i. 341.

[2] Whiting, p. 194.

[3] A couplet quoted from Ovid, in hexameter, has not been included (782-783).

[4] The most unusual rime is rich/nice (92/4).

[5] If a passage be sought to illustrate the helter-skelter riming that exists, the choice is difficult. 132-244 is one out of many.

except in that it tends to relieve the monotony of a tag at the end of every line. By the way in which quatrains overbalance the couplets, Ingelend seems to have recognized this; the continuous vacillation between one sort of verse and the other is indicative of a constant search for variety. The conclusion is that the change in riming is altogether stylistic and superficial in *The Disobedient Child* and in no wise related to the warmed-over theme of the Prodigal Son, which is the motive of the interlude.

XLVI. Like Will to Like[1]

Text: J. S. Farmer, ed., *The Dramatic Writings of Ulpian Fulwell* (London, 1906).
Date: 1561.[2]
Rhythm: light.
Prevailing metre: tetrameter couplets.

Lines:	1169	%
Dissyllabic rime:	84	7.2
Redundant rime:	30	2.6
Identical rime:	10	.9
Internal rime:	30	2.6
Latin rime:	3	.3
Unrimed Latin:[3]	1	.1
Rime lacking:	6	.5
Tetrameter couplets:	810	69.2
Tetrameter ballad-six:	143	12.2
Tetrameter quatrain:	138	11.8
Tetrameter sixain coué:	36	3.1
Tetrameter leash:	16	1.4
Tetrameter rime royal:	7	.6
Miscellaneous:[4]	20	1.7

The main portion of *Like Will to Like* is in Heywood's dramatic doggerel, but there are irruptions of various other metres that one ought to take into account before passing judgment on Fulwell's only interlude. The verse is average, and there is an abundance of song. Instead of beginning the play with rime royal, the author causes it to make a doubtful entrance when the play is nearly done, sunk in a screed of Cuthbert Cutpurse in which he bewails his wickedness,[5] a method of treatment that might have suggested to

[1] Saintsbury, i. 341.
[2] Eckhardt, i. 19.
[3] There is in addition a Latin elegiac couplet (823/4).
[4] There are two examples of the cinquain ababb (995-1009, 1131-1135) previously encountered in *Fulgens and Lucres*; see p. 16.
[5] 1142-1148.

Wapull some time later its use as a vehicle of lamentation. In place of the seven-line Chaucerian strophe there is provided the six-line ballad measure with which the play begins and, in song, ends. Throughout it appears that this correptive form of rime royal, produced by omitting the fifth line,[6] sustained the burden that had formerly fallen on its progenitor.[7]

Six stanzas of prologue are followed by vice scenes revolving about Nichol Newfangle; they employ tumbling verse.[8] Tom Tosspot ventures the first romance-six,[9] and Ralph Roister follows.[10] Couplets are resumed to sustain their share of action and dialogue,[11] and Pierce Pickpurse varies them by alternation of rime.[12] With him Virtuous Living shares the honor of quatrains,[13] later achieving the sixain in pious exhortation.[14] In the virtue scene which succeeds, God's Promises[15] and Honor[16] join Virtuous Living in extolling in this strophe what their names stand for; but Ralph Roister[17] and Tom Tosspot[18] later debase it together in their decision to steal and cut purses. Severity, the judge, speaks in sixes when he comes, armed with forensic Latin, to wreak

[6] Just as the rime royal was probably produced by omitting the seventh line from the ballad-eight. Maynard (pp. 83-92) reasonably holds that such was its genesis, and that it was not derived from the *ottava rima.*

[7] The seven-lined stanza is in truth confined to the lyrical element—in the second, third, and sixth songs. The rime royal noted above (n. 5) was probably produced by mistake, by a redundancy of the fifth line in a group of hexastichs.

[8] 37-352. A song intervenes (177-188).

[9] 353-358.

[10] 363-368.

[11] 369-609. Three songs are included (448-451, 524-527, 568-600).

[12] 610-617, 623-626, 722-729, 1149-1158.

[13] 672-687.

[14] 752-798, 869-874.

[15] 842-847.

[16] 852-864.

[17] 979-984.

[18] 985-998.

justice upon the evil-doers.[19] Cuthbert laments his lot in the same stanzas,[20] and Pierce beseeches heaven for grace in quatrains.[21] Newfangle in tailed hemistichs[22] takes the proceedings as a joke, but the Devil, as in Marlowe's *Doctor Faustus,* carries him off on his back in dramatic doggerel,[23] and Virtuous Living reflects sagely in long measure[24] upon the things which have come to pass. Good Fame at the end helps him pray for the Queen.

The interest of the playwright in his prosody is seen to have been somewhat desultory. He was intent on forsaking the ways of his predecessors to the extent of employing the hexastich, but he took the greater part of his versifying, like his title, from John Heywood. It is likely that he considered his slight flowerage an improvement on the case-hardened cantilever verse which the older writer left as his legacy to the drama. The complexity which Fulwell thus introduced is, however, of little effect. Scenes of gravity are endued with ballad-sixes, whether the character who makes use of it be of good or ill fame. It is the metre of virtue and repentance, scarcely the metre of larceny that Ralph and Tom make it. It is a facile substitute for the Chaucerian stanza which lacks its true state. The "compiler" has used it as a kind of substitute; where, for example, John Bale would have used the rime royal, for introduction, conclusion, and weighty matters with which the audience must be sent home, Ulpian Fulwell has used the hexastich, with corresponding loss to the worth of his verses.

The quatrains are intermediary between the groundwork of couplets and the superstructure of sixains. Easier to write than the latter, they proved excellent too for a substitute for the more difficult measures. It is rarely that they find employment by vicious characters, and then (except

[19] 1045-1050, 1073-1078.
[20] 1136-1148.
[21] 1149-1158.
[22] 1170-1205.
[23] 1206-1215.
[24] 1234-1241.

in scenes of repentance) only toward the beginning of the drama.[25]

In the dramatist's mind there seem to have been two categories for his versification: alternate rime for the good characters, and consecutive rime for the bad. To these two tenets he adhered scrupulously, for the most part; even the rime couée can be taken for quatrains with internal rime.[26]

Finally, the limitations of the subject have forbidden broaching the most interesting metrical question of the drama, that of the seven songs. Into these the playwright poured his greatest talent for versifying, and it may be that the entire interlude, like *Tom Tyler*, is little more than a scaffolding for the songs. The verse of these is various, and one cannot help looking at the spoken portions of this play as interstitial filler with which, as a poet, he would not so much have concerned himself.[27] On the whole, we must be content to accept the theory of closed rime for vice and open rime for virtue; arbitrary and exceptionable as it is, it is the lowest common denominator to which the dramatic portion of the verse can be reduced.

[25] The difficulties of separating quatrains followed by couplets from ballad-sixes is self-evident; the sense must choose. It may be that the author intended the whole of the spoken portion to be composed of quatrains on one hand and of couplets on the other. The liberty of taking this sixain into consideration at all is suggested by the metre of the last song.

[26] See p. 48, n. 3.

[27] Fulwell's treatise of 1575, *The Flower of Fame*, was partly in verse (text, p. 61).

XLVII. JACK JUGGLER[1]

Text: W. H. Williams, ed. (Cambridge, 1914).
Date: 1562.[2]
Rhythm: light.
Prevailing metre: tetrameter couplets.

Lines:	1062	%
Dissyllabic rime:	27	2.5
Latin rime:	4	.4
Rime lacking:	3	.3
Tetrameter couplets:	902	85.5
Pentameter rime royal:	84	7.9
Tetrameter rime royal:	70	6.6

The question of authorship concerning *Jack Juggler* cannot be irrefragably solved by this means of prosodic study, nor is its relationship with any other interludes suspected to be of the same origin sufficiently close to warrant absolutely concluding that, for example, the author of *Respublica* was also the present author.[3] Very little of the prosody, indeed, will bear discussion. Its light measures are so well wrought that it seems to be the work of a scholar like Udall, and the method of their employment is so unvaried, so even, so cloistered, that it has not the kaleidoscopic if earthy colors of the folk drama. The prologue provides pentameter rime

[1] Bradner, pp. 379-80; Brandl, p. lxi; Saintsbury, i. 341.
[2] Text, pp. vii-viii, xvi-xvii.
[3] Suggested in the text, pp. x-xvii. A composite metrical table makes this clear:

	Rime royal	Tetrameter couplets	Quatrain	Polysyllabic rime
	%	%	%	%
Jack Juggler:	14.4	85.6	..	2.5
Jacob and Esau:	2.9	97.1	..	8.4
Respublica:	..	91.0	4.3	4.5
Roister Doister:	1.5	98.0	..	9.2
Thersites:	..	76.3	4.8	12.9

royal[4] with four Latin rimes;[5] when that is concluded, "Jake Jugler" opens the play with the dramatic doggerel[6] which is never abated until tetrameter rime royal in a long passage of Careaway's serves for epilogue.[7] The rimes are good,[8] the schemes inflexible.

All things, then, connected with the versification of *Jack Juggler* point to the preceptor. He was well aware of the different kinds of verse he was manipulating, and he was able to put them into their three respective categories with the grace of a precisian. Its very perfection is its prosodic downfall. The metric stiffness, coupled with the various other tricks of Udall's style,[9] cannot fail to support the thesis that the master of Eton was its author.

[4] 1-83.

[5] 1, 2/4/6.

[6] 84-992. Pentameter seems to come partially into 550-555.

[7] 993-1062. The last line is usually a pentameter line, a kind of elongation like that which extends the last line of a pentameter stanza to an Alexandrine in *All for Money*, p. 173. In that case it occurs in the prologue.

[8] Six consecutive rimes on the same sound occur in 911-916. The worst assonances are fortune/don (991/2) and home/alone (302/3).

[9] A conclusion reasonably arrived at from the table above, n. 3.

XLVIII. King Darius[1]

Text: Brandl, pp. 361-418.
Date: 1562.[2]
Rhythm: light.
Prevailing metre: tetrameter couplets.

Lines:	1567	%
Dissyllabic rime:	59	3.8
Redundant rime:	9	.6
Identical rime:	1	.1
Internal rime:	2	.1
Latin rime:	2	.1
Rime lacking:	21	1.3
Tetrameter couplets:	872	55.7
Trimeter sixain coué:	549	34.1
Trimeter octave couée:	32	2.0
Trimeter couplets:	26	1.7
Trimeter quatrain:	24	1.5
Dimeter couplets:	8	.5
Common measure:	4	.3
Tetrameter quatrain:	4	.3
Miscellaneous:[3]	48	3.1

King Darius, as the summary indicates, is almost exclusively in couplets and rime couée. As verse it is not good. Rime is tortured that the schemes may be identifiable;[4] it appears that the unknown author merely made a leisurely stab at the old forms. The late date to which the interlude is assigned notwithstanding, the reversion to the early schemes of sixains and octaves couées make it seem a case of arrested

[1] Bradner, p. 379; Brandl, pp. lxix-lxx; Reyher, pp. 66-7.

[2] Eckhardt, i. 7.

[3] Including inchoate rimes couées (889-896, 923-928, 1050-1062), the scheme abcca (1379-1383), and the wheel measure aaaabbabbbbaaba (1224-1238).

[4] Foolish/doubtless (106/7), children/brimstone (466/7), folk/yellow (951/2), amend/warning (1008/9), head/egg (1038/9), you/magnify (1175/6), eyes/Bartacus (1444/5). These are the most amusing of the rimes, and it is seen that they are never found in the *caudae* of rime couée. Almost all belong to passages of couplets.

prosodic development. Extra lines and extra triplets[5] are to be discovered, and when rime became too much of a trial, it was left out.[6] In short, the unknown dramatist behaved toward his versification just as he pleased, and even the content of his work was treated with the same detachment. Preparatus, in a line[7] alien to the structure either of the chain of couplets preceding or the rime couée following, asks a question that is ignored. The same thing recurs later in the case of Iniquity,[8] and finally near the end even King Darius suffers a like fate:[9] his polite inquiry, "Do you intend to remain here?" is satisfied neither by rime nor words. If there were not a consistency in the omissions, of an exclusive similarity, mutilation of the text by Thomas Colwell, who printed it in 1565, would be suspected. The poverty of the character of the interlude, however, seems owing altogether to its author's incompetence.

The Prolocutor begins the drama with thirty-four lines of tetrameter couplets. Iniquity and Charity then converse in this same metre with other characters from morality plays for nearly five hundred lines, when trimeter quatrain[10] and sixain[11] follow as Equity thanks Providence for his delivery from tyranny. Couplets supervene[12] and, but for a short interruption by two servants of the king in rime couée,[13] continue until Equity exhorts the vices in trimeter rime couée to forsake their evil ways.[14] This is the beginning of a quantity of tail-rime which prevails for more than five hundred lines.[15] The allegorical characters are those that employ it; for variety Iniquity sometimes speaks in the cantilever

[5] 880-882.

[6] The percentage is comparatively high. See e.g. 1276-1278.

[7] 626.

[8] 955.

[9] 1541.

[10] 510-513.

[11] 514-519.

[12] 520-539, 587-634.

[13] 540-567. A song follows, 568-586; it too is in the trimeter sixain coué.

[14] 852-873.

[15] 852-1220.

verse.[16] Then, when Equity has finished his song of praise, tetrameter couplets are restored.[17] The rime couée of Stipator Secundus is short lived;[18] there is no reason for its existence, and the verse tumbles back. Tetrameter quatrains,[19] some in the form of common measure,[20] appear in the harangue of Zerubbabel as his emotion rises in speaking of nature and its divine government. Darius breaks in with the long doggerel,[21] and Zerubbabel in trimeter quatrains concludes his extended screed.[22] The play is then finished in rimed tetrameters.[23]

From the analysis it is inconceivable that the playwright should have had any purpose in varying the metre as he did. The only thematic manipulation of device is to be observed, if it is to be observed at all, in the use of rime couée to attract the attention of the audience to a long speech. It is slight underscoring. The exception is Stipator Secondus, and Zerubbabel's quatrains serve precisely the same purpose later in the play. Prosodically the interlude must be dismissed, for to find method in the chaos is to read more into the verse than was put there. The main thing to notice is the ground bass of couplets over which there is occasionally chanted weightier material, more or less off key.

[16] 1105-1114 with Constancy, and likewise 1140-1159.

[17] 1220-1328.

[18] 1329-1340.

[19] 1457-1525, excepting an unreasoned batch of couplets, 1474-1507.

[20] 1462-1473.

[21] 1500-1507.

[22] 1508-1523.

[23] 1526-1581. A song with refrain actually ends the interlude.

XLIX. Appius and Virginia[1]

Text: R. B. McKerrow, ed., for the Malone Society (London, 1911).
Date: 1563.[2]
Rhythm: light.
Prevailing metre: tetrameter couplets.[3]

Lines:	953	%
Dissyllabic rime:	114	12.0
Redundant rime:	7	.7
Identical rime:	2	.2
Rime lacking:[4]	4	.4
Tetrameter couplets:	407	42.7
Heptameter couplets:	368	38.6
Common measure:[5]	160	16.8
Tetrameter quatrain:	4	.4
Dimeter quatrain:	2	.2
Trimeter couplets:	2	.2

There are two kinds of verse in *Appius and Virginia*, tetrameter and septenary couplets, but it would require a rewriting of the play to make this evident. The line of separation, however, is particularly sharp and makes comment simple: for the scenes dominated by Haphazard the vice, the author has used cantilever verse;[6] and for the other

[1] Bond, p. lxxxiii; Brandl, p. lxi; Reyher, p. 62; Saintsbury, i. 342; Schipper, i. 227, 257.

[2] Eckhardt, i. 84. The conjectured author, however, Richard Bower, died in 1561 (L. Bradner, *The Life and Poems of Richard Edwards* [New Haven (Conn.), 1927], p. 50).

[3] The manner of printing must lead us to this decision, but as a true matter of fact, the septenary lines should be added to half those of the common measure, a sum which would overshadow the amount of light tetrameters (47%).

[4] There are also five Latin elegiac couplets (2-11: 1.1%).

[5] What the printer has set up as lines of common measure (riming abxb) are in reality only rimed septenaries with a consistent cæsura after the fourth stress. In the discussion which follows they cannot be considered otherwise than as heptameter couplets.

[6] 212-320, 385-408, 472-522, 559-577, 627-641, 677-684, 719-787, 999-1022, 1081-1146, 1159-1177.

scenes, i.e. those in which the main part of the drama progresses, he uses the rimed septenaries.[7] The prologue is written in Latin,[8] but the English epilogue brings the work to its termination in the lines of seven stresses.[9] For the verse itself, hypermetric lines are found in the address of Haphazard near the end of the interlude,[10] and the rimes are not clean.[11] The dramatist, however, was able to make strenuous use of internal rime in his two songs.[12]

The author of *Appius and Virginia* must therefore be considered to have separated his verse into two portions: light fours for the vice, and heavier sevens for the main history of the play. It is not possible to remark any further discrimination.

[7] The generalization is open to one or two exceptions: to the dramatic doggerel between Virginius and his wife Mater (122-158), Conscience (556), and Virginius alone (927-948).

[8] 2-11.

[9] 1205-1216.

[10] 1159-1177.

[11] Captain/begging (394/5), plum tree/country (404/5). The presence of an additional *s* of course never hinders rime, e.g. lands/befriend (793/4).

[12] 342-380, 686-717.

L. New Custom[1]

Text: J. S. Farmer, ed., *Anonymous Tudor Plays* (London, 1906), iii. 158-202.
Date: 1563.[2]
Rhythm: light.
Prevailing metre: tetrameter couplets.

Lines:	1076	%
Dissyllabic rime:	82	7.5
Trisyllabic rime:	2	.2
Redundant rime:	3	.3
Latin rime:	1	.1
Rime lacking:	5	.5
Tetrameter couplets:	1076	100.

The prosody of *New Custom* provides no occasion for delay. The verse is very light and unusually good;[3] it does not vary from the dramatic doggerel except where a line is broken off for dramatic purposes.[4] Whoever was the author of this play, he has given no second thought to change in versification: he permitted the verse to tumble along from beginning to end in the Heywoodian style.[5]

[1] Bradner, p. 379; Brandl, p. lxi; Saintsbury, i. 341.

[2] Eckhardt, i. 31.

[3] The only place in which the playwright seems to nod is in II. iii. Here are the greatest number of divagations from the *beau idéal* of cantilever couplets.

[4] II. iii. 33, 82; III. i. 147.

[5] The summary shows a great likeness in this drama to *John John,* one which is further borne out by the work of Bradner (above, n. 1) if for *thirteeners* one substitute *tetrameters.*

LI. DAMON AND PYTHIAS[1]

Text: Adams, pp. 571-608.
Date: 1564.[2]
Rhythm: light.
Prevailing metre: tetrameter couplets.

Lines:	1780	%
Dissyllabic rime:	125	7.0
Trisyllabic rime:	2	.1
Redundant rime:	20	1.1
Internal rime:	2	.1
Latin rime:	13	.7
Unrimed Latin:[3]	3	.2
Rime lacking:	142	8.0
Prose:[4]	49	2.8
Tetrameter couplets:	1379	76.6
Pentameter couplets:	288	16.1
Poulter's measure:[5]	46	2.6
Pentameter ballad-six:	18	1.0

The decision that *Damon and Pythias* is mostly in rimed prose[6] is reasonably arrived at. The play is, with a short passage of three hexastichs as the sole exception, altogether in this strange, vaguely unpleasant prose which pops in a rime at irregular intervals. The lines straggle out to twenty-five syllables[7] and dwindle to three.[8] And very often Richard

[1] Bond, pp. lxxx, lxxxii; Brandl, p. lxi; Reyher, 63-4; Saintsbury, i. 342; see especially L. Bradner, *The Life and Poems of Richard Edwards* (New Haven [Conn.], 1927), pp. 70-1.

[2] Text, p. 571.

[3] There are also two French lines (1167-1168).

[4] Groups of lines without rime and usually without cadence. In considerations of prose, however, writers have neglected these lines.

[5] In point of actual fact, the prologue contains but eight lines of this measure (1-8).

[6] R. W. Bond, *The Complete Works of John Lyly* (Oxford, 1902. 3 vols.), ii. 238-41; see also above, n. 1.

[7] 313. Other quantities of syllables in various lines are 4 (555), 18 (123, 1511, 1756), and 21 (1555).

[8] 556.

Edwards neglects to provide any rime whatever, and the metre become unabashed prose. The prologue has been said to be in poulter's measure, but there are so many consecutive lines of seven accents (when they can be ascertained) and so few of actually alternating sixes and sevens that the name is not applicable without reservation.[9] But prose it is, rimed moderately, in marked contrast to the accurate versification of the author's poems.

The ballad-sixes that alone penetrate this *mêlée* of syllables and rime belong to Eubulus, King Dionysius' councillor, chancellor, and counsellor, who in them makes his first appearance.[10] He laments the imminent fate of Pythias and deplores his inability to help alter the king's decision to put the hero to death. These lines are good pentameter ballad staves, and they are a prelude to the threnody of the Muses. Eubulus, however, does not keep up the pace he has set, and he slips down into the same prosy slough in which the rest of the characters have been mired. In sum, the only impression to be derived from the prosody of *Damon and Pythias* is one of supreme carelessness, peerless in the course of the interlude until the time when prose as such crossed it.

[9] 1-46. A song (1480-1500) is also in this measure.

[10] 1454-1471; it is reasonable to consider it as song.

LII. Horestes[1]

Text: Brandl, pp. 493-537.
Date: 1564.[2]
Rhythm: light.
Prevailing metre: heptameter couplets.

Lines:	1073	%
Dissyllabic rime:	29	2.5
Unrimed Latin:[3]	1	.1
Heptameter couplets:	614	60.8
Tetrameter rime royal:[4]	249	21.2
Tetrameter couplets:	211	18.0

The "Newe Enterlude of Vice Conteyninge the Historye of Horestes" is without a designated prologue, but the "Vyce" is first on-stage with irregular rime royal; the lines grow longer as he continues.[5] The comedy goes forward in light tetrameter couplets,[6] except for those speeches by the Vice in rime royal.[7] Horestes, hero of the piece, enters with rimed sevens[8] that do not collapse into poulter's measure. As long as he is on the stage, these fourteeners are adhered to,[9] but when he has gone, the verse tumbles back as the comic Hempstring and Haltersick "flort" each other and play the buf-

[1] Text, pp. xcv-xcvi; Bond, pp. lxxxiii, 171; Reyher, p. 62; L. Bradner, *The Life and Poems of Richard Edwards* (New Haven [Conn.], 1927), p. 51. The presence of *ottava rima* has been suggested (in the last-named place), but the strophic lines appear to fall accurately into the insular scheme of rime royal.

[2] Eckhardt, i. 85.

[3] There are also two couplets borrowed from Ovid (861-862, 888-889).

[4] Probably designed as tetrameter, but in the course of the stanzas the beats tend to increase from four to five. It is a reversible reaction.

[5] 1-21.

[6] 22-170.

[7] 38-44, 49-62, 77-108, 119-125, 146-152, 251-257.

[8] 171-188.

[9] 171-290. The influence persists until after Idumeus has gone and *Sellenger's Round* is struck up for the song of Haltersick (306-329).

foon.[10] Horestes returns,[11] bringing with him the long line, which abides with his councillors even after he has gone.[12] But for a short passage at arms between a woman and a soldier in tumbling verse,[13] the drama (as Horestes returns) continues in the septenaries, and Vice too is able to keep pace with its long stride.[14] When the fourth song has been sung,[15] Vice parodies it in rime royal whose beats gradually grow from four to five to produce on the page the same pear-shaped aspect that his prologue did.[16] The form, however, is short-lived, and the fourteeners return in the words of Fame, into which Vice makes sallies of rime royal before leaving.[17] When the stage is clear of these, Provision, Nestor, and even Horestes fall into the swing of dramatic doggerel.[18] Idumeus, however, with utter courtliness comes before King Menelaus, and the verse is once more pitched up to the lines of seven beats.[19] Horestes, general and nephew of the king, replies in the same kind of lines,[20] and the drama, but for the break of Revenge (Vice *volte face*) in rime royal of extraordinary length and vulgarity,[21] is heavily brought on to its conclusion in septenaries.[22] Truth and Duty talk about themselves and moralize in the accepted manner and in the accepted metre, rime royal.[23]

John Pikering also methodized his use of the three measures. Rime royal was reserved for the Vice, who certainly drags it in the mud. For the comic scenes, interludes,

[10] 330-399.
[11] 400-449. He soon returns to speak, 455-457.
[12] 626-647.
[13] 680-866.
[14] 718-721, 740-748, etc.
[15] 849-860.
[16] 867-887.
[17] 910-916.
[18] 926-947.
[19] 948-1037.
[20] 970-983, 1122-1163.
[21] 1038-1121.
[22] 1122-1163.
[23] 1164-1205. The number of stresses is uncertain, varying from about five at the outset to four at the end.

and various *divertissements*, the old rimed tetrameter is convenient. Finally, as the most dignified of measures under the new régime, the rimed fourteener with its double cæsura is most fitting for the speech of monarchs, and for scenes of monarchic grade this style is reserved. It is novel to find the systems of riming thus used, and most interesting to see how rime royal has been degraded. The romantic satanism which put Vice actually into the title-rôle considered rime royal as worthy of its hero, whatever he may do with it. No longer is it the king who speaks in this measure and the vice who aspires to it;[24] though he may speak with royalty in the royal rimed septenaries, royalty makes no use of its indigenous measure, and Vice has the dirty purple for himself exclusively.

[24] E.g., *The Play of the Weather*, pp. 65-6.

LIII. ALBION KNIGHT[1]

Text: W. W. Greg, ed., for the Malone Society, "Collections" (London, 1909), I. iii. 231-242.
Date: 1565.[2]
Rhythm: light.
Prevailing metre: tetrameter couplets.

Lines:	408	%
Dissyllabic rime:	6	1.5
Redundant rime:	1	.2
Rime lacking:	4	1.0
Tetrameter couplets:	328	80.3
Pentameter couplets:	38	9.3
Dimeter sixain coué:	30	7.4
Hexameter couplet:	2	.5
Miscellaneous:[3]	10	2.5

The versification of *Albion Knight,* however viewed, is not extraordinary.[4] The thirty lines of rime couée are uttered by Division, an undesirable, on entering.[5] Although there is no stage direction except that which bids him enter wearing "byll, sword, buckler, and a dagger," this bit of verse is so foreign to the rest of the fragment, so religiously syllabic in construction, and so similar in metric to the final song of *Wit and Science,* that it is most likely a song.[6] It is consequently most advisable to count this errant rime couée as song and to omit it from the corpus of *Albion Knight,* which may then be considered as written in couplets that spread from four to six beats. In thus reducing to homogeneity the metrical structure of this piece, the metre has no especial significance; most of the time the verse reads like prose rimed on occasion.

[1] Bradner, pp. 378-9.

[2] Text, pp. 229-30.

[3] Lines 9-10 cannot be scanned, and the metrical extravagance of 112, 257, 260-261, 266-268, cause them to be included here.

[4] The oddest rime is "unpossyble/quyneble" (393/4).

[5] In the *frons,* two beats; in the *cauda,* three (168-197).

[6] The last song in *Horestes* is also in this measure.

LIV. The Cruel Debtor

Text: W. W. Greg, ed., for the Malone Society, "Collections" (London, 1911), I. iv. 317-322; and (1923) II. ii. 143-144.
Date: 1565.[1]
Rhythm: heavy.
Prevailing metre: pentameter couplets.

Lines:[2]	265	%
Dissyllabic rime:	18	6.8
Trisyllabic rime:	6	2.3
Pentameter couplets:	215	81.2
Pentameter rime royal:	42	15.8
Tetrameter couplets:	8	3.0

The first half of the fragment begins in pentameter couplets, which give way to rime royal upon the entrance of Ophiletis. The first is a vice scene with horse-play among the characters already met: Flattery, Simulation, and others.[3] Ophiletis is the unfortunate debtor who, like Magnificence and Sad Circumspection in Skelton's drama,[4] bewails his misfortune in pentameter heptastichs.[5] The vices thus answer him,[6] but the approach of the king relegates him to couplets.[7]

The second part of the interlude is even more fragmentary than the first and is written in couplets exclusively. The first eight lines are in tumbling verse, and the remainder contain five stresses which tend to absorb extra syllables.[8] One can

[1] Text, p. 315.
[2] Including a line from Vergil (II. 35).
[3] I. 1-89.
[4] See pp. 36-7.
[5] I. 90-110.
[6] I. 111-132.
[7] I. 133-199. The effect which royalty has on rime royal is often queer. In some of the latter-day cases instead of the kings' conducing to this measure, it has a diamagnetic effect and they have avoided it, e.g. *A Satire of the Three Estates* and *Horestes*.
[8] II. 64 has 13 syllables, the next line 14.

do no more with this bit than to witness the existence of both rime royal for the good character fallen on evil days because of the machinations of the vices, and of rather long couplets for the scenes of action and vice. The author, like those of his time, kept his mind on varying his versification *poichè in iscena ancor le antiche maschere mette l'autore, in parte ei vuol riprendere le vecchie usanze.*

LV. ENOUGH IS AS GOOD AS A FEAST

Text: S. de Ricci, ed. (New York, 1920).
Date: 1565.[1]
Rhythm: light.
Prevailing metre: tetrameter couplets.

Lines:	1516	%
Dissyllabic rime:	178	11.7
Trisyllabic rime:	8	.5
Redundant rime:	3	.2
Identical rime:	6	.4
Internal rime:	1	.1
Unrimed Latin:[2]	1	.1
Tetrameter couplets:	900	59.3
Tetrameter rime royal:	288	19.0
Tetrameter quatrain:	272	17.9
Pentameter rime royal:	42	2.8
Tetrameter ballad-eight:	8	.5
Pentameter ballad-six:	6	.4

The metres of *Enough is as Good as a Feast* are varied to suit character. Prologus, following a tradition frequently honored, begins with thirteen stanzas of rime royal. Worldly Man, whose name is indicative of his position in the play, proceeds in quatrains. This species, the light long measure, is generally reserved for the more vicious characters like "Couvetouse the Vice."[3] From this system arises the greater part of the play in rimed tetrameter; its only apparent reason for existence is that it is easier to rime lines as they come instead of by alternation. As the play progresses and the quantity of couplets increases, reserved for the scenes of Temerity, Precipitation, and their cohorts,[4] it is possible that this kind of verse was intended for the more vicious por-

[1] Text, p. 8.

[2] A travestied Latin tetrameter quatrain (1258-1261) also exists; see n. 10.

[3] 305-352, 902-930, etc.

[4] 353-630, etc.

tions of the interlude, with rime royal for the more dignified portions, and tetrameter cross-rime acting as mediator.

This cannot be taken for a hard and fast rule. Heavenly Man and Contentation, two of the guardian-angel force that police the drama and who take Worldly Man to his death, are quite able to speak in quatrains.[5] Heavenly Man at times wedges them in between his declamations in rime royal,[6] possibly out of regard for the difficulty experienced in so speaking. Off-stage, the Prophet too is heard in quatrains,[7] although on arriving he measures his words in rime royal.[8] The words of Contentation to Queen Elizabeth at the end are naturally separated by being in ballad-six.

There can be no doubt of method in the use of the different schemes; although W. Wager is master of the several forms, including the sixain coué of the song,[9] this is not a study of virtuosity. Two factors influenced the general plan of the playwright; namely, the desire to present his characters in three steps of worth by means of the three main metres, and the facility with which these metres were written. The indignity of Ignorance's Latin gibberish shows in what disesteem the quatrain was held.[10] In spite of the comparatively great amount of rimed tetrameter, it seems to have played a slight rôle in the mechanics of the work, to have been a convenience rather than a purpose. The contrast is between the quatrain and the rime royal pedestalled on the nondescript mass of couplets.

[5] 163-166: 188-219, 238-245.
[6] 227-230.
[7] 1178-1181.
[8] 1188-1201.
[9] 281-304.
[10] 1258-1261.

LVI. Patient and Meek Grissell[1]

Text: W. W. Greg and R. B. McKerrow, ed., for the Malone Society (London, 1909).
Date: 1565.[2]
Rhythm: light.
Prevailing metre: tetrameter couplets.

Lines:	1970	%
Dissyllabic rime:	48	2.4
Trisyllabic rime:	4	.2
Redundant rime:	2	.1
Internal rime:	2	.1
Unrimed Latin:	1	.1
Rime lacking:	6	.3
Tetrameter couplets:	654	33.2
Heptameter couplets:	549	27.9
Tetrameter ballad-six:	177	9.0
Tetrameter quatrain:	141	7.2
Pentameter couplets:	123	6.3
Tetrameter rime royal:	112	5.7
Pentameter quatrain:	32	1.6
Pentameter rime royal:	28	1.4
Hexameter couplets:	7	.4
Common measure:	4	.2
Hexameter quatrain:	4	.2
Miscellaneous:[3]	141	7.2

The prosody of John Phillip's interlude is continually changing, for he had a wealth of styles at his call. There is little remarkable in his verse; tumbling verse and rimed septenaries share between them most of the action. The ballad measures are richly represented, but there is no rime couée, even in the songs. In sevens the performance is

[1] Bond, p. lxxxiii.
[2] Eckhardt, i. 66.
[3] Including the tetrameter ababxab (460-466; $x=$ an unrimed amphibrach), ababbbxb (936-943), abababcc (1305-1311), a stray leash of six lines (1596-1601), aabab (1179-1183) in the midst of couplets, etc. They are all acceptable variants from normal schemes of ballad rime.

begun with the "Preface,"[4] and they yield to the light hexastichs of Politic Persuasion.[5] There is therefore none of the usual rime royal at the beginning of the play, or indeed until it is a quarter spent; but the work is closed in this measure with the words of Post[r]emus Actor.[6] The rimes are good, but the lines have the contemporary tendency to string out hypermetrically.[7] One need find no fault with the versifying the playwright has undertaken.

Easiest of the metres to track, rime royal remains the vehicle of good. Grissell is the first to use it,[8] and it is long before anyone else has the hardihood to share it with her. Diligence the messenger is her sole rival[9] until Vulgus,[10] a character sympathetic because of his compassion on the wretched heroine, and the virtues of Patience and Constancy are granted it.[11] Even Janikell,[12] her peasant father, is at the close allowed to worry about Grissell[13] and to thank Gautier for her restoration in the Chaucerian stave.[14] No word throughout the performance is uttered in rime royal unless it has a direct bearing on Grissell, and she forbears using it except sparingly. Not only does it belong to the element of goodness in the play, but it has a further relationship to that of masochism, the ill-favoured thing which is Grissell's own.

Romance-sixes, which are ever hard to tell apart from

[4] 2-21.

[5] 2-58.

[6] 2093-2120.

[7] Especially after 1417; 1498 has nineteen syllables. This tendency is what gives rise to the intermediary Alexandrines lying between dramatic doggerel and fourteeners.

[8] 594-607.

[9] 1264-1270, 1410-1416.

[10] 1696-1702.

[11] 1787-1800.

[12] To avoid the risk of confusion, the names have been kept as they appear in the text, although the characters are better known as Griselda, Janicle, and Walter. The commoner forms are no closer to those of Boccaccio and Petrarch.

[13] 1977-1983.

[14] 2031-2037.

mere cross-rime followed by couplets, are at the outset the property of Politic Persuasion, the vice.[15] It is not, however, an unrelieved force for ill, for Grissell and her mother employ it.[16] The midwife[17] and Gautier[18] (who most normally speaks in long and dignified couplets), bitten by remorse, also uses it; and at the end of the play the ballad-six loses any significance it may have had when a general babble is put into it.[19] The quatrain, with which it is intimately linked, plus the couplet of four or five beats, is the basis on which the play is erected. It is perhaps better considered as alternate rime than as quatrain, for the way in which it is treated suggests that its appearance is due to the desire of the author to cross his rime at intervals in order to freshen his work. Properly, then, the stanzas of four lines are merely variations on closed rime and are not attempts at ballad measure.

Scenes of solemn discussion often take place in the heptameter, a manner of speaking in which Gautier is particularly at home.[20] When he strays into strophes, one is led to think that Grissell has acquired temporary dominion over him—and such is the case: she has begged a smock of him, and he has granted it her![21] Late in the play when the mood of Gautier has melted, his distant and extended septenaries diminish to the humbler dramatic doggerel, and rimed pentameter brings the end of his marital vagaries.[22]

The playwright this group of measures with motivation and dexterity. The two factions of agonism and protagonism were in his mind sharply divided, and that division was reflected in the verse which he composed. With the masculine element, Gautier and all he represents, Phillip

[15] 2-58, 81-86, 164-169, etc.

[16] 338-343, 294-305. Two lackeys likewise, 541-546.

[17] On breaking into the words of Politic Persuasion (1305-1311, 1316-1321).

[18] 1631-1636.

[19] 1971-1976.

[20] 360-365, 449-452, 638-745, etc.

[21] 1971-1976.

[22] 2038-2045.

associated rimed septenaries. With the feminine element, Grissell and the dulcet virtues, he linked rime royal in moments of flight and tumbling verse in moments of the quotidian earth-treading. The ballad-sixes appear to be the vehicle of vice at the beginning of the play, but thereafter they lose their identity in an amorphous mass of rime which is occasionally crossed. The dielectric effect of the two opposed forces of the drama is induced in the verse; as the mutual repulsion grows weaker, the verse inclines to coalesce into a homogeneous tetrametric whole. The triumph of Grissell is the decline and fall of Gautier's arrogance and dramatic personality shadowed in his verse. So closely does the change of verse parallel the change of character that one is forced to the conclusion that John Phillip was highly interested in his prosody, in suiting metre to character as it was and as it evolves. Metre is varied with a method that can only have been the result of great concern, proving exponentially valuable as time and change progress.

LVII. The Trial of Treasure[1]

Text: J. O. Halliwell, ed., for the Percy Society (London, 1850), xxviii.
Date: 1567.[2]
Rhythm: light.
Prevailing metre: tetrameter couplets.

Lines:	1011	%
Dissyllabic rime:	174	17.2
Trisyllabic rime:	2	.2
Redundant rime:	7	.7
Identical rime:	4	.4
Tetrameter couplets:	424	41.9
Tetrameter rime royal:	323	32.0
Tetrameter quatrain:	254	25.1
Tetrameter ballad-six:	6	.6
Pentameter couplets:	4	.4

The inconsequential character of this play finds its analogue in the prosody. It uses the metres which remain after the demise of rime couée[3] and the ballad-eight; the measures of four to seven lines receive their share of attention, but the main groundwork of his drama is the dramatic doggerel that was John Heywood's legacy. The seven songs are linked by a prosody that has variety, if little method in that variety. The tradition of beginning the performance with the light rime royal of four stresses, "doe all things to edifie the congregation," is adhered to, and this heptastich with the words of Time concludes the interlude. The tumbling verse is in this case broken up by the different kinds of ballad rhythm in order to obviate the charge of monotony. The thing most constant is the acceleration, the pace's rate of change.

The case for rime royal as most important of the metres

[1] Saintsbury, i. 341.
[2] Text, p. 1.
[3] Appearing hemistichically, however, in the second and sixth songs (204-214, 824-827).

is stated by Just,[4] Sapience,[5] Contentation,[6] Trust,[7] God's Visitation,[8] and Consolation[9] among the forces of good; to them it is for the most part devoted. Lust[10] and Inclination[11] occasionally err into rime royal for purposes of soliloquy, but this is exceptional use of the measure. It is recognized to be the metre of virtue and as such preserves its identity. The only example of the ballad-six is probably no more than this stave minus its fifth line.[12] It belongs to Trust, who had already been familiarizing himself with the Chaucerian strophe.[7]

Alternate rime is much less easy to transfix. On the whole, its use is more common to the vices than to their opposites; Lust,[13] Inclination,[14] Sturdiness,[15] and Greedy Gut[16] find it congenial, and the latter pair aspire to no more complex stanza. For action and for characters of less consequence than these, mere dramatic doggerel is sufficient. These categories are by no means rigid in their confines: Sapience finds not only cross-rime but couplets to his taste, and that is shared by Just, Contentation and others.

The anonymous author of this play kept the thought of his prosody well in mind, but there was no idea of distributing his metrical wares according to any inflexible principles. Uppermost in his mind was the notion of flux and change, and the identity of character which the divers measures possess is by this means reduced in clearness. He was quite able to write his light tetrapodies in the various rime schemes, and he seems to have derived a cerebral pleasure in exploiting

[4] 68-75, 78-84, 98-105, 157-171, 398-436, 661-667, 727-740.
[5] 473-479.
[6] 680-686, 691-697.
[7] 727-740.
[8] 918-943.
[9] 1064-1070.
[10] 273-279, 594-600.
[11] 316-329, 398-411. This tendency dies out as the play goes on.
[12] 1058-1063. See in this connexion p. 122, n. 6.
[13] 61-64, 105-128, 215-226, etc.
[14] 171-206, 250-253, etc.
[15] 269-272, 340-343, etc.
[16] 352-359.

each of them in turn. He seems further to have had a concept of providing the virtuous characters with rime royal and the vicious ones with quatrains and couplets. To have bound himself, however, to the exposition of these principles in cleaving one measure from the other would be diverting and fruitless pedantry; he took the various materials he had inherited, and with the practice born of long familiarity with the heritage of his theatre, he fashioned from them a smooth, polished, consciously prosodic interlude which epitomized the elements that have become classically characteristic.

LVIII. Liberality and Prodigality

Text: W. W. Greg, ed., for the Malone Society (London, 1913).
Date: 1568.[1]
Rhythm: light.
Alliteration: sporadic.[2]
Prevailing metre: tetrameter couplets.

Lines:	1296	%
Dissyllabic rime:	75	5.8
Trisyllabic rime:	2	.2
Redundant rime:	7	.5
Identical rime:	13	1.0
Latin rime:	3	.2
Unrimed Latin:	1	.1
Rime lacking:	115	8.9
Prose:	86	6.6
Tetrameter couplets:	498	38.4
Pentameter couplets:	225	17.4
Leash:[3]	99	7.7
Hexameter couplets:	72	5.6
Pentameter ballad-six:	56	4.3
Pentameter quatrain:	33	2.5
Heptameter couplets:	19	1.5
Pentameter rime royal:	7	.5
Trimeter couplets:	4	.3
Miscellaneous:[4]	201	15.5

Little of the *Contention between Liberality and Prodigality* is written in schemes other than the closed couplet. In what is actually bad verse, the lines are of no certain length, and the variations that do enter are brought in merely to suit the convenience of the author. No significance attaches to the

[1] Text, p. v.

[2] 18-38, 1298-1317.

[3] Of no consistent number of beats.

[4] Typical of the lines in this category are 1043-1048 and 1202-1206. In the first tetrameters, the rimes are distributed aaabxbcc; in the second, the beats are successively 43222, and the rimes are abaxx. For the most part, however, there is an attempt at tagging the unequal lines into prosy couplets.

way in which the beats dwindle to three[5] or swell to seven,[6] although in the latter case the additional gravity which they ought to impart would fit the words of Virtue and Equity. There is also a small amount of prose which must not be slighted. It first appears in the words of Prodigality who, having alighted at an inn, sets about awakening the host.[7] Stichomythy finds the prosaic adaptation satisfactory, and the same device is later repeated by the playwright in the fourth scene of both first[8] and second acts.[9] At the beginning of Act V[10] these forces of iniquity—Money, Prodigality, Tom Toss, and Dick Dicer—return to prose, putting it to the same use as formerly, a procedure in no way different from that of its employment in *Wit and Science* a half-century before.[11]

The measures which most claim the metrist's interest are those of ballad style, of six and seven lines. In place of the more usual Chaucerian strophe which began and ended the work of Heywood, the author of the present interlude has substituted his own staff of six lines. The prologue is wholly in ballad rhythm,[12] which runs over into the language of Vanity,[13] first of the *dramatis personae* on-stage. The play is concluded with a single stanza of this as Virtue speaks the epilogue to the Queen.[14] Its appearance within the body of the play, however, is sparing; one encounters it at the end

[5] 1212-1215.

[6] 1077-1088, 1207, 1208, etc.

[7] 66-80, 93-105.

[8] 192-198, 206-210.

[9] 379-386.

[10] 1003-1016, 1247-1273.

[11] The same is true not far from the end (1288-1297) ; see p. 60.

[12] 2-30. A stanza of orthodox ballad-six is followed by a strophe on a single rime, i.e. leash, which in turn is succeeded by one of rime royal (14-20). The one next following is the true ballad-six, but the concluding stave is shorn of its final couplet to become a quatrain. There is no ulterior poetic significance in the interchange of these various ballad measures; they are finger-exercises exclusively.

[13] 3-9, etc.

[14] 1317-1322.

of the first act in the monody of Fortune,[15] most of whose discourse is in heroic couplets. It then drops out until the fourth act is nearly over when Fortune again, vessel of power, employs it to her own advantage.[16] If there is any concrete post to which this stanza can be hitched, it is to the *dea in machinâ* whose divinity is thus exploited.

The dramatist was not, it is evident, interested in the prosody of what he was writing. Even in the songs he does not display a talent one can praise, for which he ought to have conserved his energy. Prosody and versification were not important points in the construction of his play. He acceded to the customs of the time in writing prologue and epilogue in ballad metre, with a desultory attempt or two at inserting it into the middle section of his work; but the extraordinarily large proportion of unrimed lines, the way in which they stretch and shrink, and the way in which rime is sometimes flung upon the end of short lines yoked to long:[17] all exhibit the careless attitude of the artisan toward the verse he was shaping. It is as if the notion of prosody arose into his consciousness and were immediately repressed.

[15] 269-280, 285-290.

[16] 955-966.

[17] 810/1, 891/2.

LIX. Cambyses[1]

Text: Adams, pp. 638-666.
Date: 1569.[2]
Rhythm: heavy.
Alliteration: sparing.
Prevailing metre: heptameter couplets.

Lines:	1255	%
Dissyllabic rime:	42	3.4
Redundant rime:	4	.3
Identical rime:	2	.2
Internal rime:	6	.5
Rime lacking:	9	.7
Heptameter couplets:[3]	541	43.1
Pentameter couplets:	448	35.7
Tetrameter couplets:	133	10.6
Tetrameter quatrain:	40	3.2
Hexameter couplets:[4]	36	2.9
Pentameter rime royal:	21	1.7
Common measure:[5]	12	1.0
Pentameter quatrain:	8	.6
Miscellaneous:[6]	16	1.3

The rimes in *Cambyses* are comparatively good,[7] but the lines are strung out to ever-varying lengths. Thomas Preston's prosody was not a matter for stimulating concern to him; most of the time one cannot find a standard to fit the linear size. The prologue can be said to be rimed in Alex-

[1] Bond, p. lxxxiii; Reyher, pp. 62-3.

[2] Whiting, p. 290.

[3] So varying is the syllabic texture of this type that it is best designated thus. With characteristic frequency it includes a number of examples of poulter's measure, but the happy chance that a line of six beats will precede one of seven does not justify tabulating it here.

[4] The prologue has more lines of six stresses than of fours or sevens. The variation is such that again "poulter's measure" is unwarranted.

[5] The first and third lines do not rime.

[6] Including a rimeless quatrain (247-250).

[7] There are two strange specimens of a metathetic *r*, for the sake of rime: run/turn (192/3), and thrust/durst (258/9).

andrines, in poulter's measure, or in rimed septenaries with equal justice; as a matter of strict fact, it is in all of them. The familiar dramatic doggerel grows into heptameters by syllabic intussusception,[8] and heroic couplets become pared to the tumbling tetrameter.[9] The epilogue introduces the lone example of rime royal.[10]

Ambidexter, the vice, is the first to disturb the rimed septenaries with which the play begins, and his words in alternately riming tetrameters[11] are superseded by the pentametric oaths of three "ruffins."[12] A vicious scene which embraces the king and his nobility is prosodically interrupted by the quatrains of Commons Cry,[13] but the royal scene continues in a more regal metre, septenaries.[14] Prexaspes' son[15] and Smerdis[16] give their unhappiness tongue in long measure, after which dramatic doggerel usurps the stage.[17] The murder of Smerdis is achieved, and rustic vices disport themselves until the entrance of Venus and Cupid with rimed septenaries changes the scene.[18] Ambidexter brings pentapodies back with him,[19] a metre not terminated until the queen uses common measure for what is probably a song.[20] The play is concluded with couplets, four or five beats for

[8] 551-705.
[9] 1133-1198.
[10] 1-21, p. 666.
[11] 126-157.
[12] 158-356.
[13] 357-364.
[14] 365-545.
[15] 546-549.
[16] 706-709.
[17] 710-842.
[18] 843-937.
[19] 938-1120.
[20] The text annotates the stage-direction "Sing, and exeunt" with "The song is lost" (p. 664). The context, however, plus the very great difference in versification between this portion of the play and any other part of it rather suggest that this is the song referred to. It is certainly typical of the "doleful dumps" which find their way into much of the contemporary drama.

Ambidexter,[21] and seven for the king[22] and three future oligarchs.[23]

Two general schemes of prosodic treatment may thus be discerned. The vice scenes are written in lines of four or five stresses, and the royal scenes—King Cambyses' vein—are done into rime septenaries. The two or three brief plaints in tetrastichs show the dramatist's use of this measure, exceptions to the bipartite scheme of versification. Since the dramatist was a strolling player, he cannot be supposed to have experienced great enthusiasm for the metrical meticulousness of his interlude. The senescence of rime royal was already becoming apparent, and the difficulty of its construction could easily have deterred one in his position. He versified satisfactorily in his two kinds of lines, the long and short couplets, and his distinction between them he made clear and precise.[24]

[21] 1133-1158, 1173-1186.
[22] 1159-1172.
[23] 1187-1198.
[24] See p. 131.

LX. The Marriage of Wit and Science[1]

Text: J. S. Farmer, ed., *Anonymous Plays* (London, 1908), iv. 48-100.
Date: 1569.[2]
Rhythm: light.
Prevailing metre: tetrameter couplets.

Lines:	1156	%
Dissyllabic rime:	52	4.5
Redundant rime:	4	.3
Identical rime:	2	.2
Rime lacking:	35	3.0
Tetrameter couplets:	447	38.7
Poulter's measure:	259	22.4
Pentameter couplets:	90	7.8
Pentameter ballad-eight:	80	6.9
Hexameter couplets:	77	6.7
Heptameter couplets:	58	5.0
Tetrameter quatrain:	8	.7
Dimeter couplets:	2	.2
Miscellaneous:[3]	135	11.7

While *The Marriage of Wit and Science* is obviously patterned after the work of John Redford,[4] the unknown author used other linear schemes, in keeping with contemporary tendencies. As in the earlier play, the prevailing metre is tumbling verse, but rime becomes appended to lines that swell from tetrameters to septenaries, passing through the intermediate stages of pentameters, Alexandrines, and poulter's measure. The verse itself is not good. Rime is comparatively pure,[5] but the stresses are almost impossible to

[1] Bond, p. 171; Saintsbury, i. 341; Schipper, i. 256.

[2] Eckhardt, i. 20.

[3] A nine-line leash (V. ii. 1-9) has the following system of beats: 125665556. V. iv. is more or less in couplets, but the stresses run from definite fours (40-41) through sixes (23-24, 45-46) to sevens (22, 47). All the lines in this group are irregular couplets.

[4] See pp. 60-1.

[5] After/better (II. i. 63/4), after/faster (III. ii. 22/3) are the most interesting, especially the metathesis of the last.

discern, and the necessity arises for scanning each line separately. The gradations are so fine that the most convenient way to treat these verses of rimed prose is to consider them as dramatic doggerel if the limits are at all probable.

The few breaks in the chain of couplets which links together the five acts are due to Monk's Tale stanzas. They serve as prologue before Act I[6] and reappear in the words of Nature.[7] Not until the fourth act does it return, with the words of Science,[8] who later speaks to Wit words of encouragement[9] before he undertakes the battle with Tediousness,[10] the climactic portion of the drama. There is no epilogue, and the play becomes extinguished in lines that straggle into an indefinite number of beats.[11]

Act I, a single scene, is in dignified couplets of five and six stresses for an introduction to the main business of the play Wit is given the first passage of poulter's measure[12] after the preliminary ballad-eights. The second act takes place with Wit and Will on-stage in verse that tumbles on. Poulter's measure returns in the conversation between them at the end of the second scene,[13] and the third progresses in lines of four stresses. With the entrance of Reason and Science, however, the lines become slower, changing from light fours to heavy fives,[14] and Experience furthers this lengthening.[15] In Act IV Wit,[16] Science,[17] Experience,[18] and others[19] use poulter's measure in which to elaborate on the charms of the

[6] 1-24.

[7] I. 63-105. 79 is rimeless; 80 is a monopody and rimes with a septenary, 81, before Nature's ballad-eights continue.

[8] IV. i. 92-99.

[9] V. iv. 1-16.

[10] V. v.

[11] V. vi. 14-27.

[12] I. 25-62. 52 has two beats.

[13] II. ii. 82-105. 96 has one beat.

[14] III. ii. 1-17.

[15] III. ii. 18-32.

[16] IV. i. 74-91.

[17] IV. i. 140-167.

[18] IV. i. 110-115.

[19] IV. i. 176-185.

lady Science,[16] to speak in halting accents of the incubus that is Tediousness,[17] and to determine to vanquish the same.[18] Tediousness deprecates the intended assault in the same manner.[20] The love-plaints of Wit find this their medium,[21] and so does Idleness lull him to sleep.[22] Wit, waking to find himself made a fool, recognizes the handiwork of Idleness in the same rhythm, and he bewails his fate.[23] At the end, hymeneal joys are hymned in poulter's measure.[24]

The other type of verse, more evenly written couplets, are used to fill in between the passages noted above; i.e. the playwright would break away from his steady system of cantilever verse to write a passage of poulter's measure or ballad staves, and then would revert to his old way of composition. Thus the prosody of *The Marriage of Wit and Science* is not complicated. The verse is of a consistent poverty, and it rarely changes. At intervals the dramatist appears to have realized that the opportunity for a little of his poetical by-product had come, and then to the drama it was purveyed. Beyond that, however, it is neither safe nor apposite to go.

[20] IV. ii. 1-20. 20 = "Ho, ho, ho!"
[21] IV. iv. 5-6, 22-25.
[22] IV. iv. 50-55.
[23] V. i. 1-20, 65-80.
[24] V. vi. 1-13.

LXI. Common Conditions[1]

Text: C. F. T. Brooke, ed. (New Haven [Conn.], 1925).
Date: 1570.[2]
Rhythm: heavy.
Alliteration: marked.[3]
Prevailing metre: heptameter couplets.

Lines:	1872	%
Dissyllabic rime:	28	1.5
Redundant rime:	1	.1
Identical rime:	2	.1
Internal rime:[4]	77	4.1
Rime lacking:	4	.2
Heptameter couplets:	1682	92.8
Tetrameter couplets:	52	2.8
Heptameter quatrain:	4	.2
Leash:	4	.2

The philosophical point of view is of considerably more interest in *Common Conditions* than the prosodic one. Nearly the whole interlude is done into rimed septenaries, or fourteeners, whose rimes are of the usual quality.[5] The example of quatrain is more in the style of poulter's measure, with its alternating sixes and sevens.[6] It creeps into the dialogue between the Boatswain and Common Conditions to no avail, and then is lost.

[1] Text, pp. xiv, 85; Bond, p. lxxxiii; Brandl, pp. cxvii-cxviii.

[2] Eckhardt, i. 62.

[3] Particularly noticeable when "the gear cottons," about 875, after 1275, and about 1665.

[4] The editor has pointed out (p. xiv, n. 2) the existence of an internal type of rime couée which reappears sporadically. This, the "stanza" of *The Nut-Brown Maid* (1502), is probably the measure at which the author of *Godly Queen Hester* was aiming. It consists of two lines which rime aab ccb, and the accents are distributed 2 + 2 + 3 to make up the septenary here printed. See Berdan, p. 156; Schipper, i. 367, 408.

[5] Boy/Sunday (1379/80), physician/many a one (1825/6); see text, p. 81.

[6] 1007-1010.

The shorter rimed lines of tumbling verse interrupt the fourteeners in the song of the Mariners off-stage,[7] seafarers who turn out to be pirates. As soon as they have arrived, all mystery has left them and all change has left the verse; their off-stage shouts are converted to on-stage conversation. To cantilever verse for a few brief clauses the dialogue of Clarisia and Conditions dwindles,[8] and the news that her Lord Lamphedon is well calms her anxious spirits. Stichomythia employs nine short lines to convey the excitement of Sedmond and Conditions;[9] as the tension is relaxed, the lines, like the agonists, expand. The true function of this metre, however, is not fulfilled until the entrance of Lomia, "the naturall." This unhappy madman[10] carries on his nonsense in lines of no regularity, that cannot be called tetrameter with complete accuracy.[11] Nomides speaks to him in moderately even septenaries, but Lomia, after a long silence, departs with some lines of indeterminate length.[12]

The sole conclusion which can be reached is that the author of *Common Conditions*, perhaps Thomas Preston, the player who composed *Cambyses*,[13] versified with no particular accuracy in couplets of seven stresses, and that for certain lower

[7] 983-990.

[8] 1209-1216.

[9] 98-106.

[10] L. B. Wright, "Madmen as Vaudeville Performers on the Elizabethan Stage, *Journal of English and Germanic Philology* (1931), xxx. 48-54.

[11] 1379-1428.

[12] 1491-1493.

[13] Text, pp. 83-5.

	Cambyses	*Common Conditions*
	%	%
Polysyllabic rime:	3.4	1.5
Internal rime:	.5	4.1
Rime lacking:	.7	.2
Heptameter couplets:	43.1	92.8
Tetrameter couplets:	10.6	2.8

In *Common Conditions*, however, quatrains are negligible and rime royal does not exist; see p. 159.

or more emotionally unstable scenes he cut his work down to shorter lines. His metrical interest seems confined to internal rime, as if he had picked up the trick somewhere; and there only remains to note his consistent attempt to write in the long rimed lines,[14] a rare effort in the canon of the interlude.

[14] Even prologue and epilogue are in this measure.

LXII. (Marriage of) Wit and Wisdom

Text: J. S. Farmer, ed., *Anonymous Plays* (London, 1908), iv. 258-298.
Date: 1570.[1]
Rhythm: light.
Prevailing metre: heptameter couplets.

Lines:	783	%
Dissyllabic rime:	82	10.5
Rime lacking:	95	12.1
Heptameter couplets:	280	35.8
Tetrameter couplets:	185	23.6
Pentameter couplets:	71	9.1
Hexameter couplets:	63	8.1
Poulter's measure:	28	3.6
Miscellaneous:[2]	156	19.9

"The Contract of a Marriage between Wit and Wisdom" has the same prosodic lineaments as its contemporary, *The Marriage of Wit and Science.*[3] The preponderant amount

[1] Eckhardt, i. 21; W. W. Greg, "The Date of Wit and Wisdom," *Philological Quarterly* (1932), xi. 410; Whiting, p. 143.

[2] In couplets of varying size when the verse contrives to rime; see above, p. 153, n. 3. Fair specimens are the xaaxbb accented 435224 (I. iii. 37-42), and the anarchy in rime, II. i. 24-50. The beats begin 4235... before settling into the swing of the tetrameter.

	Marriage of Wit and Science	*Marriage of Wit and Wisdom*
	%	%
Polysyllabic rime:	4.5	10.5
Rime lacking:	3.0	12.1
Tetrameter and pentameter couplets:	58.2	52.6
Hexameter and heptameter couplets:	11.7	43.9
Poulter's measure:	22.4	3.6

The results do not altogether warrant ascribing both interludes to the same author, for the most unconsciously characteristic elements of their versification, polysyllabic and omitted rime, are at great variance. See below, n. 4.

of lines with six and seven stresses in these two plays sets them apart from the rest of the interludes, a segregation which their aspect of renovation conceivably fostered.[4] The verse in each of them is extraordinarily bad, and the words of Wit in the present play belong with equal propriety to its compeer:[5]

> He hath charged me the thing to take in hand
> Which seems to me to be so hard, it cannot well be scanned.

To say that the couplet versification is in a continuous state of riot is to compose a complete epigraph. One rime in eight is omitted,[6] and into some of the scenes it is impossible to bring a respectable order.[7] The prologue begins adequately in poulter's measure and gives way to rimed septenaries of good consistency;[8] and these are the verses which terminate the interlude[9] after a final bit of poulter's measure.[10] *At in medio asperrimus ibis.*

It is hard to believe that the dramatist had any definite notion of changing his prosody when he wrote some scenes in fours and others in sixes and sevens. Idleness speaks in rimed septenaries in both his own character[11] and that of Honest Recreation.[12] Wit,[13] Wantonness,[14] and Wisdom[15] also make use of them. The strained tone of the talk in dramatic doggerel[16] before the battle between Wit and Irksome-

[4] Adding together all the lines of six and seven stresses would show an even closer approximation: *The Marriage of Wit and Science*, 34.1%; *Marriage of Wit and Wisdom*, 47.5%.

[5] I. ii. 47-48.

[6] Especially in II. i. 24-49. This laxity is rivalled only by the early "Enterlude of Youth" (13.6%), and is approximated in *Liberality and Prodigality* (8.9%).

[7] I. iii. 37-122.

[8] I. i. 1-68, I. ii. 1-10.

[9] II. vi. 47-65.

[10] II. vi. 41-46.

[11] I. ii. 1-10.

[12] I. ii. 75-80.

[13] I. ii. 47-58; I. iii. 123-139, 214-217.

[14] I. ii. 147-160.

[15] I. iii. 177-182, 185-211.

[16] I. iii. 212-213.

ness becomes changed to the long heptapodies when Irksomeness has been beaten.[17] The cutpurse scene is in particularly bad verse,[18] and Idleness has throughout a peculiar facility for destroying the metrical equilibrium.[19] But conscientiously varying the prosody the author was; whether it was one Francis Merbury or another, his wretched verse-forging takes place in a continuum of third-hand drama. He has true need of the apologetic conclusion, "For, though the style be rough . . ."[20]

[17] I. iii. 214-217.
[18] I. iii. 1-73.
[19] Especially in II. i. 1-79.
[20] II. vi. 58.

LXIII. Abraham's Sacrifice[1]

Text: M. W. Wallace, ed. (Toronto, 1907).
Date: 1575.[2]
Rhythm: mixed.
Prevailing metre: pentameter couplets.

Lines:	891	%
Dissyllabic rime:	28	3.1
Redundant rime:	3	.3
Internal rime:	2	.2
Rime lacking:	5	.6
Pentameter couplets:	703	79.0
Tetrameter couplets:	172	19.3
Trimeter couplets:	12	1.4
Trimeter quatrain:	4	.4

Except for the four little lines of alternate rime,[3] the "Tragedie of Abraham's Sacrifice" which Abraham Golding translated from the French of Théodore de Bèze is exclusively in couplets. This departure from the traditions of interlude writing can be attributed to the French original,[4] whose verse goes from Alexandrines to tripodies. The corollary to this is the lack of a prologue prosodically distinguished, and of an epilogue.[5] In Golding's work both of these are set somewhat apart by being written in heroic couplets. The author has achieved some renown as a poet, and this untragic morality play does nothing to diminish his fame. In an almost line-for-line translation of Bèze's work, he expected to conserve the French theologian's metre as much as practicable. So far did he carry this idea into practice that those cases in which French tetrameter is rendered into English pentameter are noteworthy.

[1] Text, pp. lx-lxi.
[2] Text, pp. 1-2.
[3] 250-253.
[4] Bèze had approached the subject of metrics in his treatise on pronunciation published at Geneva in 1584, *De Francicae linguae recta pronunciatione* (repr. Berlin, 1868).
[5] See p. 161, n. 14.

It is for this reason impossible to appraise the metric elements of *Abraham's Sacrifice* accurately. We are not now dealing with an original in which the poet has free rein, but with a copy in which he must submit to all kinds of trammels, and in which versification becomes a *tour de force*. Bèze, in writing his *tragédie,* had no acquaintance with the English popular stage of the sixteenth century, and his mode of writing had nothing in common with that of it. From the prosodic point of view, the present interlude is not an English work at all, and one which can find no place within the scope of such a survey. Its traditions are French and its form is French, rather jejune as we see it. No profit could arise from a catalogue of the way in which the variously sized couplets are used even if a system for varying them could be discovered. There is no prosody to account for.

LXIV. The Glass of Government[1]

Text: J. W. Cunliffe, ed., *The Works of George Gascoigne* (Cambridge, 1910. 2 vols.), ii. 6-90.
Date: 1575.[2]
Rhythm: heavy.
Prevailing metre: pentameter quatrains.

Lines:[3]	363	%
Latin rime:	1	.3
Pentameter quatrain:	128	36.3
Pentameter rime royal:	119	32.8
Heptameter couplets:	40	11.0
Pentameter ballad-six:	36	9.9
Poulter's measure:	34	9.6
Pentameter couplets:	6	1.7

George Gascoigne conceived his interlude in prose.[3] The verses that appear in it are comparatively few, and their purpose in existing is perspicuous. As in the older interludes, prologue and epilogue are differentiated from the rest of the drama by means of verse, the former in iambic pentameter quatrains,[4] and the latter in pentameter rime royal.[5] The verse too is perfectly wrought: the rimes are good, the alternation of stressed and unstressed syllables is mathematically sound, and the fluency of words, though cold, retains its clarity. Its chiselled aspect permits none of the usual variations in metrical construction; there is no evidence of linkage, of extraneous or redundant rime, or even of dissyllabic rime. This, if poor poetry, is excellent verse, and as good verse it must be considered.

The alternate rime of the prologue is concluded with a couplet before the comedy is allowed to proceed. Verse does not return until "The first Chorus," in pentameter rime royal, moralizes to the audience with a liberal dosage of *auctoritee*

[1] Macdonald, pp. 469-70.
[2] Whiting, p. 244.
[3] The 2525 lines of prose are excluded; see p. 211, n. 71.
[4] Text, p. 6.
[5] Text, pp. 88-90.

from the ancients.[6] At the end of Act II the second chorus serves its function in the metre of the prologue.[7] Before the third act has been got ready for the chorus, two portions of verse are spoken by Phylotinus and Phylomusus respectively. Phylotinus puts into rimed septenaries the counsel that his instructor had given him in prose, dogmata that were intended to be impressed upon the audience.[8] The avowed purpose, however, is to display his "simple skill in poetry," and Phylomusus counters with alternately riming pentameters to instruct all who attend to their duty toward the king, ministers, magistrates, etc.[9] Ballad-sixes this time prove the chorus' vehicle to extol the fruits of early industry.[10]

The chorus at the end of Act IV makes use of the infrequent poulter's measure in which dodecasyllabics alternate with tetrakaidekasyllabics;[11] and at the end of Act V, Epilogus, on "What soever is written, is written for our learning," takes the place of a concluding chorus.[12] It is in the true Chaucerian stave of five linear stresses.

The composition of this interlude in prose, a situation that was not to find its equal in the scope of our discussion, gives rise to a wholly new use of verse. It was a general use of verse, not of specific types, like those that are to be found in the play which compass it round about. It is as if any kind of verse would do; the agrestic poulter's measure is not deemed inferior to the aristocratic rime royal. The variety of the verse indicates that Gascoigne, a literary athlete who left no event from his list, considered these little tags to his play as exercises and essayed nearly as many forms as he felt he could manage. As far as accuracy of expression is concerned, his success has already been acknowledged; but his verse remained beyond the actual pale of his drama, and he used it without internal significance. It became merely a concluding convenience in which he could practice his skills.

[6] Text, pp. 26-7.
[7] Text, p. 43.
[8] Text, pp. 55-6.
[9] Text, pp. 56-8.
[10] Text, p. 59.
[11] Text, pp. 70-1.
[12] Text, pp. 88-90.

LXV. THE TIDE TARRIETH NO MAN[1]

Text: E. Rühl, ed., *Shakespeare Jahrbuch* (1907), xliii. 13-52.
Date: 1576.[2]
Rhythm: light.
Prevailing metre: tetrameter quatrains.

Lines:	1811	%
Dissyllabic rime:	128	7.1
Trisyllabic rime:	4	.2
Redundant rime:	2	.1
Identical rime:	4	.2
Latin rime:	6	.3
Unrimed Latin:	2	.1
Rime lacking:	5	.3
Tetrameter quatrain:	945	52.7
Tetrameter couplets:	558	30.8
Tetrameter rime royal:	196	10.8
Dimeter sixain coué:	102	5.6
Trimeter couplets:	4	.2
Trimeter quatrain:	4	.2
Heptameter couplet:	2	.1

This "moste pleasant and merry commody, right pythie and full of delight. Compiled by George Wapull" is constructed mainly in four different types of verse. Wapull kept his prosodic conscience in hand, as a bare outline of the use of these metres will illustrate. The versification is, on the whole, rather good; it points to the unusual regard of the poet for the manner in which he was to write his play. It commences legitimately in the light rime royal with a prologue,[3] a scheme not duplicated at the end, which contrives unobtrusively to taper off with the cross-rime of Christianity.[4] Since the writer was so much aware of his metres, it is good to look at their employment *seriatim*, and to see how they fit the matter they expound.

[1] Text, pp. 10-11; C. F. T. Brooke, *The Tudor Drama* (Boston, 1911), pp. 115-6.

[2] Text, p. 12.

[3] 1-56.

[4] 1872-1879. The quatrains begin at 1828.

The drama begins with the entrance of Courage the Vice, chanting his Skeltonic rimes couées.[5] Other vices join him in cantilever verse[6] which continues until Greediness and Courage argue in alternate rime.[7] Their dialogue returns to the tumbling doggerel with the entrance of two more vices, and the lot of them make merry with a specious hedonism.[8] Courage brings urbanity and quatrains with him as wickedness has its way.[9] Rime royal supervenes with the appearance of the "Tenaunt Tormented," a sympathetic character whose ruin has been brought about by Courage.[10] His lament is superseded by more tumbling verse when Wanton and Courage frolic together.[11] The vein remains the same until Courtier, stripped of his goods, returns to bemoan his fate in the Chaucerian stanza.[12] He is mocked by Courage and the others who have undone him, in couplets[13] with a break of alternate rime.[14] Wastefulness cuts the verses to Skeltonics,[15] but it soon recovers, swelling to heptameters by way of atonement.[16] The style of verse remains that of consecutive rime with occasional intercalations of cross-rime until Debtor, in the gripe of the police, speaks his sad mind in rime royal.[17] The verse dwindles as they depart, whereupon

[5] 57-158.

[6] 159-346. A song intervenes (291-311).

[7] 347-427.

[8] 428-587.

[9] 588-793.

[10] 794-835.

[11] 836-1081. The scene between Courage and Wanton, as the commentators have noted (see n. 1) is written in lines which rime by fours (836-967). It is an unusual scheme of rimes, but beyond its being unique there is no more to be said. Hurtful Help speaks in alternate tetrameters (968-995), and Courage sings a song in the meantime (1028-1052).

[12] 1082-1116.

[13] 1215-1226.

[14] 1117-1214.

[15] 1227-1230.

[16] 1245-1246.

[17] 1393-1404. 1405/6 do not rime. A third song is also wedged in (1337-1358).

Christianity enters[18] and is assisted by Faithful[19] in the manufacture of rime royal for self-revelation. Their respective monologues concluded, they converse in alternate rime,[20] a quatrain each, setting wrong things right, unravelling the iniquitous skein of the unfortunate. The *dénoûment* is morally satisfactory; Correction takes Courage, the agonist, off to jail after a brief bout in the rimed tetrameters.[21] Faithful, Christianity, and the Author ruminate together upon what has passed, and the interlude terminates with an invocation for guidance in quatrains.[22]

Rime royal, except for its use in the prologue, is seen to be used exclusively for the expression of dolor, for laments at having been beguiled into the paths of vice. The metre is somewhat redeemed at the end by Christianity's use in soliloquy, but it remains as if it were the most lyrical of the measures and best adapted to the complaints of the evil days on which the protagonists have fallen. Their doleful dumps sound best attuned to the Chaucerian stave, while the staple of verse is the rimed light tetrameter, usually consecutively, occasionally in alternation. The rime doggerel at the very beginning is for the induction of Courage as chief villain of the piece, and it never reappears. The reasons for Wapull's use of these different measures seem to be clear: rime royal for lyrical lamentation, dramatic doggerel for the bulk of the play, and cross-rime for the sake of varying the sound. If this study of measures does nothing more, it shows that Wapull was perfectly cognizant of the different schemes, and that he endeavored to enliven his work by changes in versification.

[18] 1440-1467.
[19] 1468-1488.
[20] 1489-1811.
[21] 1812-1827.
[22] 1828-1879.

LXVI. All for Money[1]

Text: E. Vogel, ed., *Shakespeare Jahrbuch* (1904), xl. 146-186.
Date: 1577.[2]
Rhythm: light.
Prevailing metre: tetrameter couplets.

Lines:	1572	%
Dissyllabic rime:	82	5.2
Redundant rime:	4	.2
Internal rime:	10	.6
Latin rime:	20	1.3
Unrimed Latin:	4	.2
Rime lacking:	10	.6
Tetrameter couplets:	438	27.9
Pentameter couplets:	402	25.6
Pentameter ballad-six:	210	13.4
Pentameter rime royal:	210	13.4
Pentameter quatrain:	84	5.4
Tetrameter quatrain:	48	3.1
Common measure:[3]	28	1.8
Tetrameter rime royal:	21	1.3
Hexameter rime royal:	14	.9
Hexameter ballad-six:	12	.8
Miscellaneous:[4]	94	6.0

The sole work of Thomas Lupton exhibits great diversity of metre. Couplets, quatrains, and ballad measures of the different types are all to be found in various array. So great is the diversity of metre that it is felt to be achieved at the expense of good versification. Rime is not good[5]—when it contrives to exist—and lines are omitted at irregular intervals. The whole sensation derived from looking at the pros-

[1] Text, pp. 140-2.

[2] Eckhardt, i. 33.

[3] Riming abxb.

[4] With variation like the pentameter ababcdceeff (152-163) and ababcdd (289-293), and various couplet appendages to the rimes royal and quatrains.

[5] Appeareth/health (117/8), is/wish (273/4), manners/father (497/8), riches/increase/diminish (722/4/5).

ody of *All for Money* is that it was written all for speed and variety, and that good versification was disregarded.

The drama begins in the pentameter rime royal with bad rimes.[6] These are exceptional stanzas, for they adopt the extraordinary expedient of introducing an extra foot at times into the last line, after the fashion of the Spenserian stanza.[7] This rich and strange alteration in the case of Spenser (whose "February Eclogue" in *The Shepherd's Calendar* is not beyond the reproach of doggerel[8]) becomes in the hands of Lupton a ridiculous trick. It ceases with the prologue,[9] but the Chaucerian strophe continues under the ægis of Theology until Science finds it difficult to keep the metre going any longer,[10] and lapses into a leash of five beats.[11] Rime royal appears sporadically in the mouth of Art,[12] but more especially Theology.[13] In the meantime Money has arrived, and he chants in a sort of common measure to emphasize his less dignified and noble bearing,[14] and Adulation, who follows him upon the scene, offers him homage in the pentameter couplet.[15] In couplets the dialogue proceeds until Pleasure interrupts with an inaccurate rime royal stanza.[16] These undesirables and others, Sin and Pressed For Pleasure, restore couplets[17] with slight interruptions[18] and proceed to the words of Damnation in the Chaucerian strophe.[19] In long

[6] 1-140.

[7] The elongated lines are most particularly 14, 28, 42, 70, and 84. See Maynard (pp. 118-120) concerning the rime royal with concluding Alexandrine. Sir Thomas More was the first, apparently, to use this device.

[8] Saintsbury, i. 353.

[9] 8-84.

[10] 141-144.

[11] 145-148.

[12] 164-170.

[13] 175-181, 192-198.

[14] 203-230.

[15] 231-256.

[16] 289-293, riming ababcdd—at a venture. As the editor notes, a line seems to have been lost between 292 and 293.

[17] 294-371.

[18] 372-375, 395-398.

[19] 399-405.

fourteeners the vices greet his self-presentation and presently depart.[20] Sin soliloquizes at length in lengthy lines[21] broken by cross-rime only for the sake of variety[22] and a snatch of rime royal with which he concludes his smug appraisal.[23] Satan enters with couplets to bandy words with Sin,[24] and after a fit of weeping and roaring bewails his infernal lot in heptastichs.[25] With intervals of cross-rime the vices carry on their complots;[26] Satan, agreeing to make them sport, uses the Chaucerian measure.[27] Money Without Learning, and Learning Without Money, oddly enough, continue to use the same easy doggerel as the rest,[28] and the seven-line stanza does not come again until Learning Without Money speaks of the consolation and great riches of his scholastic attainments.[29] Except for this brief encomium, the play goes forward as before to its conclusion with only four more staves of ballad-seven. The first of these belongs to Sin, whose guile is not abated.[28] The second underscores the entrance of Gregory Graceless, who has just gained £200 as a footpad.[29] For the next five hundred lines cross-rime shares the drama with cantilever verse until the end of the performance is at hand. Goodly Admonition enters with an Alexandrine rime royal that has a weighty imperial effect.[30] Three sobering

[20] 406-413.

[21] 414-445.

[22] 446-471.

[23] 472-478.

[24] 479-568. The alternate rimes cannot be said to have significance. Pride uses them with some frequency (493-496, 503-506, 545-548), but he also speaks in the pentameter couplet (485-486, 549-550). The same is true of Gluttony.

[25] 569-582.

[26] 618-720.

[27] 721-727.

[28] 930-936.

[29] 1035-1041.

[30] 1526-1546. There are but three beats in the first of these lines, but those following soon make up for it. The verse grows more and more tumid; 1532 has nineteen syllables. As the play ends, it is an uncertain reminiscence of the Prologue, who also swelled his rimes in this fashion. The author must be given credit for a conscious purpose in thus infusing syllables into his scheme.

stanzas of this verse and the author relapses into the simpler schemes of vice, while Virtue, Humility, and Charity assist Goodly Admonition.[31] A final stanza to him[32] and Lupton has done, whittling his play into a prosodic anti-climax befitting so uninspired a work.[33]

From this metrical summary it is hard to find any unity in the dramatist's utilization of schemes. Quatrains dip in and out to vary the monotony. The whole attitude of Thomas Lupton toward the work he put together with apparent abandon seems careless. He made an attempt at the beginning and end to mark out the head and tail of the piece with rime royal, but that was the sum of its purpose. Sin, Satan and Damnation wield it just as well as Goodly Admonition. Since the dramatic unity of action is unbroken, vice having its merry way throughout, the formal metre has no reason for appearing when it does. It probably comes because the rimes happened to suggest themselves to the writer. Relief from the mass of couplets now often characterizing the later interlude seems to have been Lupton's only motive in alternating rimes; this is easier to do, and there are more of them: but as far as the verse is concerned, *All for Money* is a raucous *vox et praeterea nihil.*

[31] 1549-1556.

[32] 1557-1563.

[33] 1564-1572. One heroic stanza is followed by riming lines of 14-16 syllables.

LXVII. The Three Ladies of London[1]

Text: J. P. Collier, ed., *Five Old Plays* (London, 1851), pp. 159-236.
Date: 1582.[2]
Rhythm: light.
Prevailing metre: heptameter couplets.

Lines:	1608	%
Dissyllabic rime:	95	5.9
Trisyllabic rime:	2	.1
Redundant rime:	16	1.0
Internal rime:	2	.1
Rime lacking:	37	2.3
Prose:	14	.8
Heptameter couplets:	1114	69.4
Tetrameter couplets:	427	26.6
Hexameter couplets:	59	3.7
Pentameter couplets:	4	.2
Tetrameter, abxb:	4	.2

The versification of *The Three Ladies of London* is a portent and a warning. Each line must be scanned by itself, and when the scansion is done, one has nothing. The lines are irregular in length[3] like those of *Damon and Pythias*, and this interlude too is easily called rimed prose. The rimes are bad.[4] On looking back through this play, the only things to note are the comparative lengths of the lines that rime. Nor does there seem to be any reason for certain lines to be longer than others. Dissimulation,[5] Fraud,[6] Simplicity,[7] and Tom[8] all use the old tumbling verse; but on the other hand,

[1] Macdonald, p. 470.

[2] Eckhardt, i. 23.

[3] 196 has six syllables; 261 has twenty-four. It suggests some of the humorous verse of today; see p. 2, n. 4.

[4] Him/eating (692/3), alike/seek (1407/8).

[5] 34-41.

[6] 101-111.

[7] 123-133.

[8] 1353-1356.

all are capable of speaking in longer lines,[9] so that no conclusion can be reached from their diverse characters. There is no connexion between the nature of a scene and the length of the lines in which it is cast. The little prose of Mercadore signifies nothing,[10] and the stichomythia of Peter and Simony[11] is a return to the device of Wit and Science.[12] The small quatrain of fours by Fraud[13] means nothing either; probably it is the result of chance. The conclusion one draws is that Robert Wilson the elder, author of this interlude, gave not a thought to its prosodic construction, thinking that when he had put in a rime he had done with the technics of his verse. This is rimed prose, and to consider it as anything more is futile.

[9] Dissimulation speaks in septenaries after 399; Fraud uses hexameters after 65; Simplicity in octameter after 1524 and Tom with Will employs seven stresses after 1333.

[10] 396-397.

[11] 806-812.

[12] *Wit and Science*, text, 453-542.

[13] 1520-1523.

LXVIII. The Three Lords and Three Ladies of London[1]

Text: J. P. Collier, ed., *Five Old Plays* (London, 1851), pp. 249-346.
Date: 1588.[2]
Rhythm: heavy.
Prevailing metre: blank verse.

Lines:	2452	%
Dissyllabic rime:	20	.8
Redundant rime:	6	.2
Identical rime:	9	.4
Internal rime:[3]	2	.1
Rime in blank verse:	116	4.7
Rime lacking:	46	1.9
Prose:	680	27.7
Blank verse:	1107	45.3
Pentameter couplets:	230	9.4
Tetrameter couplets:	192	7.8
Leash:[4]	43	1.8
Pentameter rime royal:	42	1.7
Pentameter quatrain:	16	.7
Latin prose:	7	.4
Miscellaneous:[5]	92	3.9

A later companion-piece to *The Three Ladies of London*, this drama pays far more attention to metrical structure. Although nearly three-quarters of it is in prose and blank verse, the remainder is in well formed schemes that illustrate the concern of the playwright with his versification. The prologue, which in *The Three Ladies of London* was spoken in rimed fourteeners, in this play marks a return to the old ways of rime royal.[6] Lady London speaks this before the interlude begins in blank verse, and the measure does not

[1] Macdonald, p. 474; Saintsbury, i. 342.
[2] Eckhardt, i. 24.
[3] Line 892 has a curious double internal rime, aabb.
[4] Usually in tetrameter (scattered between 90 and 102, 425-429, etc.).
[5] For instance, abccdefff (1207-1215).
[6] Text, p. 249, 1-21.

recur[7] until the end of the play when Pomp, one of the three Lords, prays for blessings on Queen Elizabeth.[8] All, however, is concluded in pentameters of alternate rime with the words of Pleasure, the third Lord.[9]

The three Lords first enter to begin the drama in blank verse,[10] which they continue to speak throughout its length.[11] Their pages—Wit, Wealth, and Will—use the old dramatic doggerel for their comedy,[12] but its use is not exclusive, for they relapse into prose at times.[13] The indigent Simplicity shares the tumbling verse with them,[14] and it returns spasmodically with the vices Fraud, Usury, Simony, Dissimulation, and their fellows.[15] The middle section of the play is free from tetrameter couplets; they do not reappear until Policy, the first Lord, brands Usury with a hot iron; and even in this passage their tendency is to stagger into lines of seven beats.[16] In this same style the prothalamion is written to be sung by "a wench";[17] a colorful dance follows before the departure of the three Lords with the three Ladies (Love, Lucre, and Conscience) for the cinematic culmination. Nemo remains behind like a chorus to comment, in pentametric rime royal,[18] on the events that have come to pass, tying up all the threads that the audience may have overlooked. After two stanzas of this Chaucerian measure, Nemo ("a grave old man") makes his further observations in quatrain,[19] the form that had hitherto been used only for the heroines near the beginning.[20] Hemistichic cross-rime savoring of John Skel-

[7] Except in the words of Nemo (2335-2348).

[8] 2426-2432.

[9] 2435-2438.

[10] 1-89 (text, pp. 251-4). 33-35 are in prose.

[11] 470-502, 1120-1200, 1439-1459, 1694-1883, 1954-2039, 2201-2228.

[12] 90-127, 357-365, 409-448.

[13] 128-158, 366-407, 449-469.

[14] 357-365, 409-448.

[15] 801-804, 828-845, 857-904.

[16] 2076-2095.

[17] 2328-2334.

[18] 2335-2348.

[19] 2349-2352.

[20] By Love (663-666) and Lucre (671-674).

ton belongs to the banter that flies back and forth between the Lords and Ladies and serves merely to put an edge on their flippancy.[21]

Once more, between prose and blank verse there are no clear-cut lines to be distinguished. For the most part, the respectable characters use blank verse[22] and the villainous persons speak prose.[23] Prose is also available for the Spanish of Fealty[24] and Spanish Pride[25] as well as for their Latin,[26] and its virtue in stichomythia[27] cannot be compared with that of blank verse, for example. Prose is a good vehicle for Painful Penury and Simplicity,[28] in contrast to which the dignity of Nemo and the three Lords is well served by rimeless pentameter.[29] The general tendency so to constrict the use of the two preceding modes of expression can be noted, but the prosodic conscience of Wilson kept him to no strict differentiation. The two kinds of writing with a discrimination easily fatigued, like his ability in writing rime royal.

The consequence is that on perusing this interlude the reader is persuaded to feel that the schemes had established themselves in the playwright's mind, and that he desired to cast his work into these forms in accord with the characters to whom the lines were given, but that by the time he had written the first quarter of the drama, his strength of purpose failed, and he fell into the easier ways of alternating prose

[21] 1201-1204.

[22] Blank verse is used by the heroines Conscience and Love (647-650), by Fealty (1666-1689), and by Shealty (an Irish word equivalent to "liberty," 1694-2039). It is not immune to Fraud (739-762) or Usury (846-856).

[23] Fraud, Usury, Simony, and others speak prose in 561-646, 785-800, 905-909, 1336-1438, 2040-2075, 2229-2327. In this last case the hero Policy is held in thrall by Fraud; other scenes in which the Lords are degraded by vice to prose are in talk of war (1460-1482), and with Fraud and Simplicity (2377-2423). Two Lords, Pomp and Pleasure, speak prose together in 2096-2200.

[24] 1691.

[25] 1690-1953.

[26] 1692-1693, 1884-1885.

[27] 1003-1007, 1914-1920, etc.

[28] 1059-1119.

[29] 1120-1200.

with unrimed verse. In the last hundred lines of the play he seems to have taken his prosody in hand once again and to have bent his energy to more complex versification so that the close might be worthy of the polychromatic substance of the drama. One is precipitated into a maelstrom of all but rime couée.[30] The two great divisions still hold, and this is the only impression with which one is left on having finished: that but for the desultory attempt to vary the versification at the beginning and end, Robert Wilson was content to write the words of his heroes, heroines, and those of their rank in blank verse, and that the others must get along in prose.[31]

[30] Its last appearance had been in *The Tide Tarrieth No Man* at least twelve years before. Couplets and the ballad staves of four and seven lines are to be found in this last *pot au feu.*

[31] In summarizing, one can also say that the scenes in which one class of character predominates are written in the appropriate measure, that even when the forces of evil use the blank verse which belongs to their betters, it is because they are of more than ordinary significance, and that the author is preaching to the audience in his "pleasant and Stately Morall." On the other hand, he is capable of preaching in pentameter couplets and cross-rime at the end of his interlude. To any formulated rule there cannot fail to be exceptions; Wilson's use of prosody seems to have been subject to constant change like the slope of an harmonic curve whose points of inflexion cannot be determined. See p. 188, n. 9.

LXIX. The Peddler's Prophecy

Text: W. W. Greg, ed., for the Malone Society (London, 1914).
Date: 1590.[1]
Rhythm: light.
Prevailing metre: tetrameter quatrains.

Lines:	1584	%
Dissyllabic rime:	196	12.7
Trisyllabic rime:	6	.4
Identical rime:	2	.1
Latin rime:	1	..
Unrimed Latin:	3	.2
Rime lacking:	18	1.1
Linkage:	2	.1
Prose:[3]	7	.4
Tetrameter quatrain:	1333	84.2
Tetrameter couplets:[2]	181	11.4
Pentameter rime royal:[2]	63	4.0

The Peddler's Prophecy is constructed on comparatively orthodox prosodic lines; its verse is not so bad as that of Robert Wilson's[4] other work. At its worst it is really no more than prose printed as verse, of which there are examples enough in the Tudor interlude. There is no impossible complexity of schemes as there is in the other "prophetic" play, *The Cobbler's Prophecy*, and the attention to writing well of the matters at hand has made this a piece of good workmanship. Rime is good,[5] and the lines contrive to stay rather well within the bounds with which four accents hedge them. The prologue is in pentameter rime royal, which becomes altered in the first scene to dramatic doggerel. Alternate rime plays a large part in the metrics of this play as it did

[1] Eckhardt, i. 78, n.; see below, p. 211, n. 71.
[2] Of indeterminate beats and number of syllables.
[3] Accepting the thesis that he is the author; see text, p. v.
[4] See below, n. 10. Macdonald has by exclusion treated it as verse.
[5] The worst are seventh/heaven (200/2), and handled/mangled (1472/4).

in those of W. Wager, *The Trial of Treasure*, and *The Tide Tarrieth No Man*. When it becomes time to conclude the drama, the Peddler speaks in quatrains and not in rime royal, for none of it overflows the prologue.

Tumbling verse first appears in the words of the Prologue[6] and later becomes established when the Peddler opens the first scene.[7] When the "mayd" enters, she brings long measure with her,[8] and it carries through song[9] and over a stretch that is difficult to classify.[10] A scene later ensues in which the Peddler again speaks in closed rime,[11] but this is soon overpassed by a long passage of alternate rime, with which the play ends.[12] The dramatic doggerel seems reserved only for scenes of more or less reverent diversion, while the drama itself belongs in quatrains.

Thus one cannot say that Wilson was so careful of alternating his metres as his rimes. He composed, once he had written the prologue, almost exclusively in quatrains. Sufficiently aware of his metrics to change over twice to the dramatic doggerel, he must therefore be given credit for a desire to vary his measures to lend additional interest to his work. That it failed to take him far is not important; it must be concluded that he was only moderately interested in metrics at the beginning of his conjectured career as playwright. The sharpness of the cleavage lines and the simplicity of prosodic variation make it comprehensible and unified, two qualities of which his later work stood in great need.

[6] 2-78. 37-50 are not in strict form, for they rime abbccddeeeff, more like couplets.

[7] 90-141. The Peddler really begins the scene in trimeter, groaning 81-89.

[8] 143-1089.

[9] 462-469.

[10] 813-819. This can be taken like the quatrains above if the lines be considered to have respectively 14, 14, 17, and 11 syllables; see n. 4.

[11] 1091-1191. The forsaking of any attempt at all to provide a rime for "Nabuchodonozer" (1190) must inevitably call to mind Jonathan Swift's provision, "The curse of God be on you, sir!"

[12] 1193-1592. Two lines of rimed tetrameters break in (1571-1572) as they had once before (79-80).

LXX. A Merry Knack to Know a Knave[1]

Text: J. P. Collier, ed., *Five Old Plays* (London, 1851), pp. 353-421.
Date: 1592.[2]
Rhythm: heavy.
Prevailing metre: blank verse.

Lines:	1833	%
Dissyllabic rime:	3	.2
Identical rime:	20	1.1
Rime in blank verse:	173	9.4
Prose:	370	20.2
Blank verse:	1441	78.7
Tetrameter couplets:	10	.5
Tetrameter, abxb:	8	.4
Pentameter couplets:	4	.2

In the last decade of the sixteenth century the influence of the Elizabethan stage came to make itself felt upon the last stragglers of the popular drama. Rime has, to all intents, disappeared. Honesty in *A Merry Knack to Know a Knave* attempts to revive the old dramatic doggerel, but his effort is brief;[3] and when he concludes the play, it is with heroic couplets after a session of blank verse.[4] Alternate rime enters only by mistake.[5] The rest of the work is prose and a blank verse frequently dashed with rime. Perhaps it is blank verse; most likely it is nothing more than sheer prose printed as "vers libre," and the whole play would profit by being reset altogether as prose.

The King, Edgar, and his friends begin in blank verse;[6] a view of the first few lines will give a fair prospect of the kind of verse that the author has blanked: rime appears

[1] Macdonald, p. 478.
[2] Eckhardt, i. 259.
[3] 1695-1704.
[4] 1830-1833.
[5] 1822-1829.
[6] 1-80.

gratuitously in the tenth line, and the fifteenth has sixteen syllables. The blank verse has a propensity for swelling to eight or more beats.[7] Prose is spoken by the Broker,[8] the Poor People,[9] the Priest,[10] the King,[11] the Madmen of Gotham,[12] and even Honesty.[13] What is sinister is that Conycatcher speaks the best blank verse of all.[14] Honesty,[15] the Farmer,[16] Bishop Dunstan,[17] Perin (a courtier),[18] Ethenwald,[19] the Priest:[20] all employ this measure too, tumescent to bursting at times. From this analysis no formulation of reasons can be made for the playwright's change from one metre to the other. No one will question the wisdom of having the Madmen speak, like Lomia,[21] in prose,[22] or of having Conycatcher's down-going attended to in prose,[23] whereas it is to be expected that bishop, priest, and king deserve blank verse if there is any. Piers Plowman speaks in prose with the King,[24] but the Farmer is permitted to use blank verse.[25]

The only sensible conclusion to be reached is that the dramatist did not attend to his prosody. Whenever con-

[7] About 134 and 135; also on p. 380, lines 1146-1158 *et passim.*

[8] 595-598, 630-656.

[9] 935-1025.

[10] 1536-1601.

[11] 1159-1164.

[12] 1319-1361. See Macdonald (above, n. 1) and L. B. Wright, "Madmen as Vaudeville Performers on the Elizabethan Stage," *Journal of English and Germanic Philology* (1931), xxx. 48-54.

[13] 1766-1773, 1783-1799.

[14] 599-629, 657-699.

[15] 1800-1821, 802-934.

[16] 1026-1036.

[17] 1146-1158, 1602-1694.

[18] 1165-1183.

[19] 1362-1527.

[20] 1705-1766.

[21] See p. 160.

[22] Although for the purposes of prosodic analysis Lomia's mad words are taken to be in tetrameter couplets, they are in reality merely prose, with rime for spasmodic satisfaction.

[23] 1783-1799.

[24] 1184-1233.

[25] Above, n. 15; 1026-1036.

venient, he suited prose to the more earthy characters and verse to the more exalted ones. Since he so often forgot to take the versification into account and wrote what may by some without further ado be considered pure prose, one cannot seek and find a wrought plan in metrical construction. What change there was was unconscious; a subtle feeling for propriety moved him to generalize in these two forms, but the basis on which he made his assignments was less concrete than spectral.

LXXI. The Cobbler's Prophecy

Text: A. C. Wood and W. W. Greg, ed., for the Malone Society (London, 1914).
Date: 1593.[1]
Rhythm: mixed.
Prevailing metre: tetrameter quatrain.[2]

Lines:	1631	%
Dissyllabic rime:	14	.9
Trisyllabic rime:	2	.1
Redundant rime:	4	.2
Rime in blank verse:	92	5.6
Rime lacking:	32	2.0
Prose:	418	25.7
Blank verse:	405	24.8
Tetrameter couplets:	137	8.4
Pentameter couplets:	92	5.6
Common measure:	80	4.9
Heptameter couplets:	49	3.0
Pentameter ballad-six:	30	1.8
Tetrameter quatrain:[3]	16	1.0
Hexameter couplets:	12	.7
Short measure:	4	.2
Miscellaneous:[2]	389	23.8

The Cobbler's Prophecy is metrically irregular to such an extent that one does not easily feel justified in analyzing it according to any of the usual schemes; it can ill afford it. With its complement of song, with a quarter each of prose, blank verse, and disorderly quatrains, with its lines that yaw into rime without felicity: the play is evidently an olio with-

[1] Eckhardt, i. 77.

[2] These miscellaneous schemes are all more or less in the style of tetrameter quatrains. Most striking are the splattered quatrains aab b x b (if the space be used to denote the end of the printed line; 639-652). Other specimens are the slightly tetrametric aaabcbdeff (62-75), abaaaccddeeffggxxhh (117-136), abbcbdbefgfchih... (91-107), and the wheeling measures aabbbb (309-314) and abaacaa (653-661).

[3] Printed as such.

out plan. There is no true prologue: Ceres begins the action in blank verse;[4] and when the time has come to conclude, blank verse is again the medium.[5] The versification is poor; the lines swell from two to five stresses[6] or even seven[7] without provocation, and the blank verse is far from indefectible.[8] As poetry, the work of Robert Wilson is not worthy of detailed consideration, and even his prosody provides little to lure the student to positive satisfactory conclusions.[9]

The prevailing metre of the drama is really prose. It first arrives in the conversation between the Scholar, Courtier, and Country Gentleman with Ralph Cobbler.[10] The prose is mellifluous, pointing not a little toward *Euphues* of John Lyly in the next five years. The loftier aspects of this prose are neutralized by the less serious quips and cranks of Ralph, who makes fun of the Soldier[11] and enters whooping at another time with "Waha how, wa how, holla how

[4] 1-31.

[5] 1234-1244.

[6] 496-498.

[7] 668-673.

[8] 959-991. A rime accidentally occurs, 989/90.

[9] The tabulation of Wilson's metrically analyzed characteristics is thus:

	The Cobbler's Prophecy %	*The Peddler's Prophecy* %	*The Three Ladies of London* %	*The Three Lords and Three Ladies of London* %
Polysyllabic rime:	1.0	13.1	6.0	.8
Tetrameter and pentameter couplets:	14.0	11.4	26.8	17.2
Hexameter and heptameter couplets:	3.7	...	73.1	...
Tetrameter and pentameter quatrains:	30.7	84.2	.2	.7
Rime royal:	...	4.0	...	1.7

[10] 222-308.

[11] 499-522.

whoop. . ."[12] The deleterious effect which this sort of thing can have on versification, and the virtue of relegating it to prose, is easily observed; it represents the most flagrant case of Wilson's use of unmetrical lines. It is a proper carrier for the comedy that the hero brings to his rôle.

The more weighty parts of the play are presented in blank verse, sparse in the early sections but thickening as the work goes on. The Soldier (Sateros) uses it for sententious observation,[13] and it seems connected more with his meditative moments during the first six scenes of the drama. Contempt and Venus, however, find it to their fancy in their comments on the Soldier, whose amatory side they brood on,[14] and in their treatment of Mars.[15] In this measure[16] the play comes to an end in a manner which suggests Wycherley's *The Country Wife*. The result one derives from such notes is equivocal; the only thread which can link together the playwright's uses of the rimeless pentameter is military, and such a tie provokes a strain in the achievement.

There are a few staves of ballad-sixes, two consecrated to Thalia,[17] Muse of Comedy and Bucolic Poetry, and the others to Ennius the Courtier[18] in his dithyramb on villainous ambition. Both passages occur rather close together; once the dramatist had written these stanzas, he took his leave of this style. They are an interesting interpolation.

The lavishly sprinkled quatrains are connected with Mercury,[19] Ralph, the Muses, and various other characters.[20] Their purpose is to vary the metre from the usual closed rime, and it easily becomes converted into rimed septenaries,

[12] 608-613.
[13] 435-444.
[14] 821-847.
[15] 886-905, 921-931 (with the Soldier), 997-998, 1025-1091.
[16] 1128-1185, 1234-1244.
[17] 585-596.
[18] 698-733. 712 is the only third line that rimes as it ought. The other stanzas rime abxbcc.
[19] 138-193. Ralph soliloquizes, however, in heroic couplets, 179-189.
[20] 570-581.

so that the two are at times indistinguishable.[21] The customary five to seven beat lines fill in the gaps between prose, blank verse, and the various other examples of alternate rime as they had done in the previous interludes.

Like the substance of the play, prosody too proves disappointing. The bad verse is badly handled and changes without reason. The words of Pride in *Godly Queen Hester* might profitably be borrowed by way of peroration:[22]

> All this is out of season, and nothing done by reason,
> Nor yet by good ryme.

[21] 664-673, 748-750, 762-784, etc.
[22] Text, 484-485.

LXXII. Summer's Last Will and Testament

Text: A. B. Grosart, ed., *The Complete Works of Thomas Nashe* (London, 1885. 6 vols.), vi. 85-170.
Date: 1593.[1]
Rhythm: heavy.
Prevailing metre: blank verse.

Lines:	1973	%
Identical rime:	7	.4
Latin rime:	2	.1
Unrimed Latin:	15	.8
Rime in blank verse:	63	3.2
Prose:	923	46.7
Blank verse:	1042	52.8
Tetrameter couplets:	12	.6
Pentameter couplets:	10	.5
Miscellaneous:[2]	9	.5

Last of the interludes, the play of Thomas Nashe is free from the artlessness that characterizes the folk drama. There are no more echoes of the complicated rime schemes with which the first of the interludes, not yet a century ago, had appeared. The entire prosody of this play, save for the interesting songs it contains, is in a virtually monochromatic blank verse. The metric of the prose, which constitutes nearly half the play, does not belong to this study, and that of the blank verse, unless one is to treat it in the manner of the late laureate of England, is not rewarding.[3] The rimed pentameter that does appear is due to the presence of alien rime. The only examples of native rime are to be found in the pentameter couplet that creeps into Harvest's dissertation on Gleaners,[4] and in the last will and testament

[1] Text, p. xxxiv.

[2] Consisting of the occasionally undistinguishable prose and blank verse. This small limb of the play can without injustice be added to the body of the prose.

[3] R. Bridges, *Milton's Prosody* (Oxford, 1921).

[4] 947-948.

which Summer reads[5] at the end of the play before the satyrs and hamadryads carry him off. The heroic couplets receive short shrift, and it is not long before blank verse reasserts itself. Before leaving the question of rime, it is also well to point out that the dramatic doggerel finds its last reverberation in Nashe's work, in the words of Will Summer chanted[6] toward the end of the *dramma per musica.*

In the cycle of prose and blank verse there is, of course, method. Will Summer the fool is wisely restricted to prose[7] like the homelier characters Harvest,[8] Bacchus,[9] and Christmas.[10] The seasons, however, speak in verse throughout. Of the old traditional prologue which one might be led to look for—since Thomas Nashe so patently set out to write an interlude styled, like the rest, "a pleasant comedie"—there is no trace. The play commences with the prosing of Will Summer and ends with his epilogue. In this work the poet had no occasion to feel the necessity for writing poetry to embody prosodic principles, as did those who wrote thirty years before. To be acted once before the Queen, perhaps by the "little eyases" of *Hamlet,* and then forgotten:[11] such was the fate in store for the drama, while the lyrics could easily continue to sing themselves far and away. The author cannot have felt any incentive to vary the metrics of his work; it lacked all interest for him, and he paid it very little heed. The very carelessness of his prosodic approach is attested by the amount of strayed rime. Nashe was a complete Elizabethan, and most of the Elizabethans deserving of the name were notoriously lax in the "normalisation" of their poetry.

* * *

[5] 2002-2009.
[6] 1883-1894.
[7] 1-129, 248-251, 470-497, etc.
[8] 887-892, 908-920, etc.
[9] 1061-1136, 1143-1178 (except Winter's blank verse, 1150-1151).
[10] 1753-1802, 1812-1862.
[11] Text, pp. xxx-xxxiii.

There now remains to bind the various strands together. The group of interludes covers an entire century, a span twice as large as that of the great Elizabethan drama, and the difficulty attendant on reducing this cycle of interludes to a homogeneity is apparent. Their chronological scope begins in the reign of Henry VII. and embraces virtually the whole of the Tudor ascendancy.

The question of Continental influence can satisfactorily be dismissed.[1] Bede's principles concerning rime had become well established in the course of seven centuries;[2] complicated verse structures had bloomed and withered.[3] The overseas emphasis on syllabic uniformity was distinctly felt in the realm of lyric poetry, but in dramatic poetry the lines went their merry hypersyllabic ways.[4] There was a fair degree of consistency concerning the number of beats in each line, but the number and position of unstressed syllables was utterly irregular, a situation incompatible with the Latin treatises of the twelfth and thirteenth centuries.[5] Of all the men in whom the traces of mediæval Latin might be expected

[1] There is no evidence to show that those who wrote the plays under consideration were acquainted with the treatises of Matthieu de Vendôme (see L. Bourgain, *Matthaei Vindocinesis Ars Versificatoria* [Paris, 1879], and E. Faral, *Les Arts poétiques du XII*[e] *et du XIII*[e] *siècle* [Paris, 1924], pp. 13-4, 109-93), Evrard l'Allemand (see Faral, op. cit., pp. 38-9, 337-77; and G. Mari, *I Trattati medievali di ritmica latina* [Milan, 1899], pp. 453-62; see also Patterson, i. 17-8), or even John Garland (see Berdan, pp. 125-6; Mari, op. cit., pp. 407-52; Patterson, i. 18-9; E. Habel, "Johannes de Garlandia, ein Schulmann des 13. Jahrhunderts," *Gesellschaft für deutsche Erziehungs- und Schulgeschichte Mitteilungen* [1909], xix. 1-34, 118-130; G. Mari, "Poetria magistri Johannis anglici de arte prosayca metrica et rithmica," *Romanische Forschungen* [1902], xiii. 883-965). For a discussion and bibliography, see Patterson, i. 13-96; ii. 4-10, 18-58. The only extent to which the scholastic tradition (see Berdan, pp. 120-229) affected the verse in the interludes was in its scansion by stresses rather than feet as linear units.

[2] Patterson, i. 14.

[3] See p. 4, n. 13.

[4] Brooke, p. 116.

[5] See Faral, op. cit.; W. Meyer, *Gesammelte Abhandlungen zur mittel-lateinischen Rythmik* (Berlin, 1905. 2 vols.); G. Paris, *La Littérature française au moyen âge* (Paris, 1890), pp. 199-200; U. Ronca,

to be found, the likeliest is John Skelton, poet laureate of Oxford, Cambridge, and elsewhere;[6] but his sole interlude betrays no more constraining familiarity with such principles than any other.[7]

This thesis is further borne out in the Latin plays of this period, for instance in the work of Nicholas Grimald and John Foxe, to mention but two authors.[8] Their work is done as a matter of pedagogy in classical Latin metre without a vestige of mediæval sophistication. To remain even within the pale of the Tudor interlude, the treatment of the Latin one does find is not suggestive of any foreign influence from Besalú to Machaut.[9] For the rest, what Latin is quoted in the plays is in the metre of the classics, hexameters in general; and although the playwrights had no qualms in riming Latin with English as the monks had rimed it with other Latin, one cannot attribute this humorous and macaronic versification to the treatises of France, Provence, and Italy.[10] The complicated tricks and schemes which their

Cultura medioevale e poesia latina d'Italia (Rome, 1892. 2 vols.), i. 319-61; E. H. Sturtevant, "Commodian and Mediæval Rhythmic Verse," *Language* (1926), ii. 223-37. See also Berdan, pp. 120-8.

[6] See pp. 4, 7, 39; Berdan, p. 93; L. J. Lloyd, "John Skelton and the New Learning," *Modern Language Review* (1929), xxiv. 445-6; H. L. R. Edwards, "The Dating of Skelton's Later Poems," *Publications of the Modern Language Association* (1938), liii. 602, n. 6.

[7] The Continental Latin tragedies of the Scot Buchanan do not deserve consideration in this connexion; it may, however, be remarked in passing that his work at Bordeaux is almost contemporaneous with that of John Bale at the see of Ossory.

[8] Berdan, p. 351; J. M. Hart, "Nicholas Grimald's Christus Redivivus," *Publications of the Modern Language Association* (1899), xiv. 369-448; C. H. Herford, *The Literary Relations of England and Germany in the Sixteenth Century* (Cambridge, 1886), pp. 113-9, 138-48; L. R. Merrill, *The Life and Poems of Nicholas Grimald* (New Haven, 1925). See further A. Harbage, "A Census of Anglo-Latin Plays," *Publications of the Modern Language Association* (1938), liii. 624-9.

[9] Patterson, i. 13-70; ii. 4-10, 18-58.

[10] Two passages among the interludes come to mind with regard to the presence and influence of mediæval Latin. The first of these is in Sir David Lindsay's *Satire of the Three Estates*, indigenous to Edin-

ingenuity devised[11] affected the systems of riming no more than did the syllabic rigidity of the theorists, and our dramatists were moved neither by Continental precept nor example in their versification. It seems most likely that they were subject to no external influence whatever.

The most important conclusion derived from a prosodic consideration of the interludes is ancipital and has already been heralded in the introductory section. It is concerned with the construction of the verse and with the use the dramatist made of the verse he had constructed. The verse is of the doggerel kind, with a general attention to the number of stresses in the line and a vague attention to the number of unstressed auxiliary syllables. The mensuration of the lines in most cases was a matter of beats and not of syllables.[12] In the dramatic portions of the verse, i.e. exclusive of the song in accordance with past practice, the attention of the dramatist was not directed toward an impeccable syllabic system of linear construction. Even at the risk of repetition, it is necessary to appreciate the light in which the writers conceived their plays and accordingly to judge them.

The kind of verse and the forms into which it fell have already been treated in the prefatory matter, but the salient point of conclusion is that the author of the Tudor interlude was almost invariably conscious of his prosody and interested in varying the verse-forms he inherited. This is almost universally true, and the exceptions are quite noticeable. *The World and the Child* is the first drama to fall away from the standard of variation set by Medwall, in which the characters of good speak in rime royal and those of evil make use of

burgh, which has ever been a fortress of Latin. Two stanzas of a mediæval lyric are quoted outright (4609-4616; see p. 75). The second harking back to the Latin of the Middle Ages comes in the parody of Bishop Bale in *King John* (633-634):

> Sancte dominice, ora pro nobis
> Sancte pyld monache, I beshrow vobis!

These two citations are of no consequence but furnish an interesting sidelight on this question of Latin.

[11] Patterson, ii. 59-452.

[12] See p. 3. Bradner's counting of syllables is also relevant here. See also Berdan, pp. 145-7; Hendren, pp. 28-31.

rime couée. The lack of significance in metric variation may be in great measure due to the quantity of alliteration with which it is pervaded; but it must be recalled that however little significance the playwright attached to the alternation of measures in *The World and the Child,* he did vary them to a great extent.

The notion that rime couée better befitted the scenes of madcap activity, and that ballad measures of six, seven, or eight lines were better suited to those of a more serious nature was one which took firm root in the ground of the secular drama whence it drew its strength. In *Fulgens and Lucres* the lines of demarcation are sharply drawn; in *Nature* they are still to be discerned. *Wealth and Health,* which begins as the playwright chooses, becomes steadied from the middle onward in the familiar partition of measures. The reverse of this is true of Rastell's play, *The Four Elements,* in which his interest in keeping one kind of verse for one type of episode and another kind for the similarly other type lapsed with the progress of his poesy, and he settled lazily into a congenial rut of tail-rime.

The two dramatic excrescences of *Hickscorner* and *Youth,* belonging to approximately 1512, betray no interest on the part of their nameless authors in the versification of their work. The great variety of measures in the first is balanced by the paucity of them in the second; the plays have little in common. *Magnificence,* done a few years later, the last play (it is probable) to be written before John Heywood brought Promethean fire to the interlude, also does away with the strictures of Medwall. Rime royal loses its halo and becomes reserved for words of direct address to the spectators while the action, which is forced to wait for the end the declamation, is carried forward in riming lines.[13]

The fire of John Heywood, however, consumed the inherited two-fold prosodic pabulum of his predecessors, reducing the alternation of measures to a light ash of rimed lines containing four beats. *The Pardoner and the Friar* and *Witty and Witless* mark the departure from the old

[13] See pp. 35-9.

paths,[14] a procedure followed through *The Four P's, John John,* and the probably Heywoodian *Gentleness and Nobility.*

Godly Queen Hester escaped the influence of Heywood and reverted to the canons of Medwall by employing a consciously varied prosody: rime royal for the serious portions, rime couée for the vicious portions, and the light rimed tetrameter to bridge the gaps. The unchanging rime royal of *Calisto and Melibea* and *Robin Conscience* of the *annus mirabilis* of the interlude, 1530,[15] is parallelled by the lack of importance attaching to the rimes of *The Prodigal Son,* the changeless cantilever verse of *Gentleness and Nobility,* and the increasingly alliterative verse of *Temperance and Humility. Wit and Science* endeavors to withstand the apathy that has befallen metrical variation; systematically it begins, with vice confined to rimed hemistichs and Skeltonics, but the enthusiasm of Redford for maintaining his scheme is soon permitted to flag.

A change of attitude toward the uses of verse marks Heywood's later play, that of *The Weather.* Jupiter speaks in rime royal, the more important of his suppliants are endued with cross-rime, and the scenes in which Merry-Report is the centripetal force are written in the dramatic doggerel: the whole is a conscious attempt to fit the verse to the character. *The Play of Love* varies the verse in another fashion: Love's Philosophy is expounded in rime royal, and the four-beat doggerel is used for the passages in lighter vein.

Before coming upon the controversial plays of Bishop Bale, the influence of Heywood on *Thersites* is to be noticed; the play is in rimed lines of from two to five beats. John Bale's *Three Laws* employs rime royal for scenes of dignity and virtue, heroic couplets for its staple of verse, and rime couée for the nefarious activity of Infidelitas. Rime royal is used in *God's Promises* as it was used by Skelton in *Magnifi-*

[14] Five concluding strophes are addressed to the audience for sage counsel.

[15] Also the year of Wynkyn de Worde's song-book, the first one to be printed in England. It contained twenty songs of three and four parts and fragments of twenty others; they have been reprinted by E. Flügel, *Anglia* (1889), xii. 585-97.

cence, to moralize and to address the audience, but the action of the drama takes place in rimed pentameters. Variation in prosody is not of great importance in *John the Baptist*; the element of divinity and the words of the author share rime royal between them. *The Temptation of Our Lord* recalls the *Three Laws.* Rime royal is first given to the protagonists and rimed tetrameter to persons of lesser stature; the reservation of measures, however, is not preserved, and the play comes to its actual end in dramatic doggerel. In *King John,* Bale's last and greatest drama, rime royal is used for the key characters and for passages of a reflective nature; no moral discrimination is connected with its application.

The bulk of *Jacob and Esau* is in the cantilever verse of Heywood, a procedure which Luke Shepherd followed in *John Bon and Mast Parson. Somebody Avarice and Minister, Jack Juggler, Respublica, Roister Doister, Albion Knight,* and *New Custom* bring this tradition to its conclusion in the history of the interlude about 1563.

The bad verse of *Tom Tyler and his Wife* is without significance, nor is there any reason for the use of the different measures of *The Disobedient Child* except for the added interest that variation must bring. *Lusty Juventus,* on the other hand, returns to the antique customs of Bale and of Heywood's forerunners, lending tail-rime to vice—in this case Hypocrisy, who addressed the audience with exhortation in rime royal—while bestowing the heptastich upon the more important characters, and in cementing the whole with couplets. *The Nice Wanton,* which might have preceded them by a few years, is also ordered in this way, and alternate rime is added as a vehicle for the scenes in which good strives with ill.

Mary Magdalene begins with the allotment of dramatic doggerel to the vicious element in the drama at the beginning, but when cross-rime appears, it is destined to remain. No significance, however, attaches to them, even in those plays like *The Longer Thou Livest, the More Fool Thou Art* in which it predominates.[16]

[16] See pp. 182-3; 208, n. 49.

The year of Richard Tottel's *Miscellany*[17] may have marked a reversion to alliterative verse in *John the Evangelist.*[18] The custom of expressing good in ballad-measure, evil in tail-rime, and binding the work together with rimed tetrameters was revived. *Impatient Poverty* begins in this style, but before long the playwright has lost his hold upon prosodic variation, and a mad syndrome of rimes is the result.

With *Cambyses* rimed septenaries first appear, devoted to royal scenes. Preston has distinguished sharply between them and the scenes of vice, which are done into riming lines of four and five stresses. The same pattern is employed in *The Conflict of Conscience,* save that for couplets are substituted whole stanzas of rime royal.

Like Will to Like marks a coming back to the old system in which grave scenes of either good or ill character are written in ballad measure, the good and virtuous *dramatis personae* are given quatrains, and the wicked are vouchsafed the common dramatic tetrameters.

King Darius is without prosodic significance; it is merely in bad verse, while *Appius and Virginia* follows *Cambyses.* The vices employ the light tetrameters, and the history of the tragedy is carried on by heavier riming lines of seven stresses.

The rimed prose of *Damon and Pythias* speaks for itself in muddy accents like that of *The Three Ladies of London. Horestes,* its contemporary, institutes a new variation of Medwall's principle in accordance with more modern theories of prosodic change and an employment of septenaries in place of rime couée which had, with *King Darius,* almost departed from the interludes.[19] By a strange perversion rime royal has become the property of vice while the monarch and persons of consequence use the long sevens, and tumbling verse remains the property of the comic element. Pikering's

[17] Berdan, pp. 343-4; Bond, p. xc; see also below, p. 202, n. 24.

[18] 1557 is the date usually assigned to it (Eckhardt, i. 29; Whiting, p. 116); the earlier date suggested by the editor (see p. 40, n. 1) has been accepted for present purposes because its earliness seems to fit its analysis.

[19] See below, p. 207, n. 46.

prosodic conscience is followed by that of W. Wager in *Enough is as Good as a Feast*: cross-rime is for the vices, rime royal for those who are clothed with dignity, and cantilever verse for a mediating influence.

The complexity of *Patient and Meek Grissell* is occasioned by the extraordinary interest of Phillip in the mechanics of his verse. The influence of Gautier is borne on rimed fourteeners, that of Grissell and virtue on rime royal, that of vice in ballad staves, and the little everyday matters on dramatic doggerel. The association of verse with character and influence is worked out with the skill of Wagnerian *Leitmotiven.*

The Skeltonic application of rime royal to the laments of "hem that stode in heigh degree" finds echo half a century later in *The Cruel Debtor.* Action and the vices make use of rimed lines. *The Trial of Treasure* is loosely constructed on the principle that rime royal is the property of virtuous scenes and that tumbling verse fits those of vice, a primordial treatment reminiscent of Bale and indicative of the future *The Tide Tarrieth No Man.* In the latter play rime royal is the verse-language of sadness and lamentation; the rest is in dramatic doggerel relieved by great amounts of alternating rime.

Wapull's metric vigilance is exceptional during the fifteen years following *Liberality and Prodigality* (1568). The calisthenics of Gascoigne are, to be sure, an exception to virtually everything in the Tudor interlude; his poetic infusions are beyond the *materia prosaica* of the actual play. From *Liberality and Prodigality* to the advent of blank verse in 1588 with *The Three Lords and Three Ladies of London,* the playwrights showed little interest in change of versification.[20] Differentiation is here made only to the extent that the villainous element speaks prose and the more respectable persons of the drama employ blank verse.

[20] This is true of *The Marriage of Wit and Science,* the *Marriage of Wit and Wisdom, Common Conditions* (which is wholly in septenaries), *Abraham's Sacrifice* (see pp. 165-6), *All for Money,* and *The Three Ladies of London.*

Caste is the determining factor in *A Merry Knack to Know a Knave* as to who may speak prose and who blank verse; but the author paid little heed to drawing an exact social line. *The Peddler's Prophecy* betrays slight effort to vary the measures, and there is no attention paid to prosodic alteration in *The Cobbler's Prophecy*. In Nashe's pastoral, *Summer's Last Will and Testament,* the more serious characters, like the seasons, use blank verse, and Will Summer, with Harvest, Christmas, and Bacchus, enjoy themselves in prose: the distinction, however, is not of great importance.

The brief recapitulation which precedes will show to what degree the dramatist busied himself with metrics, not only *per se* but in relating it to the matter of the play. Starting from 1497,[21] the two—drama and verse change—go hand in hand until John Heywood made away with prosodic significance.[22] Bale restored the coupling of metrical change with what took place on the stage, but the easier style of Heywood, which sank the drama in a sea of doggerel tetrameters, found many imitators in the years which followed. The coming of septenaries in 1569 lent another handle to the machinery of versification, and the result followed that the writers of interludes once again took stock in suiting the verse to the character and to the nature of the episode.

For a few years, perhaps eight, the interest was maintained, occasionally with grave scruples, but thereafter Saintsbury's term "prosodic anarchy" is particularly appropriate. Blank verse banished the more complex schemes from the repertory.[23] If one takes into account that interludes had been written in rimed prose and that now rime too may be dropped, the effect of the licence is obvious. There had been little evenness in the blank verse of the *Æneid* which

[21] The *Interludium de Clerico et Puella* must be considered only a kind of foreword; see pp. 14-5.

[22] He nevertheless returned to the customs of the *bon vieulx temps* in his later plays of *The Weather* and *Love.*

[23] A. Schröer, "Ueber die Anfänge des Blankverses in England," *Anglia* (1881), iv. 5-37.

appeared in 1557,[24] especially if it be so unfairly compared with the elegant and subtly varied metre of *Paradise Lost*;[25] certainly no strides had been made over dramatic terrain during the intervening quarter-century. With all metrical barriers down, then, it is to be expected that distinction in verse will pass from the drama, and this is indeed the case. At the end one is left with a heritage of prose and blank verse that does not suggest its ancestry, or with a mixture of rimes that signify nothing.

The history of the various rhythms that make up the interludes begins with the elementary distinction between heavy and light.[26] In surveying the plays one can look only for those which are predominantly in one form or the other and disregard the various smaller denominations: ours must be a majority opinion. The whole subject of heavy and light rhythm is one to which an objective approach is difficult, and the results are shadowy. In general, however, the interlude was written in light rhythm, i.e. there was an extravagance of unstressed syllables.[27] It is the exceptions to this generalization which are noteworthy. *The Droichis Part of the Play* is the first to have an appreciable amount of heavy verse.[28] *A Satire of the Three Estates* contains a large quantity of it, like *The Old Man and his Wife* later prefixed. When septenaries first trod the boards, they brought a heaviness that was, however, not invariable; *Appius and Virginia* excellently utilizes the contrast between the heavy lines of seven beats and the light lines of four whose actual size presents no great disparity. In this case too it has significance, but one which appertains more probably to the case of the seven monopodies rather than to the want of unstressed

[24] Books II and IV were translated into an English form of Latini's *verso sciolto* by Henry Howard, Earl of Surrey; see Berdan, pp. 354-60; Saintsbury, i. 314-6; Schipper, ii. 256-64.

[25] The work of Robert Bridges has already been mentioned, p. 191, n. 3.

[26] See p. 21.

[27] In contrast with the English doggerelized tetrameters there come to mind the contemporaneous *Redondilhas* of Luís de Camões.

[28] See pp. 14, 220.

syllables. The preponderance of long lines in *Common Conditions* produces a similarly weighty effect, a specious ballasting. The condition is naturally continued in *A Merry Knack to Know a Knave* because of its blank verse, and with *Summer's Last Will and Testament* the wheel is brought full circle.

Of the plays indigenously heavy in verse, it must be noticed that they are preëminently of Scottish origin. An interesting phenomenon, reasons cannot here be propounded for it, for they would entail an historical discussion of Scottish metrics.[29] We can but notice the iambic tread as more or less characteristic of the Stuart interlude, ascribe it to what we will.

The critical point of alliteration[30] as a factor in the versification of the interlude is also a difficult matter. There was little of it in 1300 and less in 1497 when Medwall was producing his work. *The World and the Child* is the first to exhibit this element to a marked degree, and in this case it works havoc with the orthodox measures. In Skelton's *Magnificence* it is like another string to the poet's bow of great strength, and it is abundant in the earliest of Heywood's plays, *Witty and Witless.* For a decade it drops from sight until its reappearance in *Temperance and Humility,* in which it acts like a wedge, gradually inducing itself more and more as the work proceeds. *A Satire of the Three Estates* is pronouncedly alliterative, like *The Old Man and his Wife.* Head-rime, as it has been called, strays at times into *John Bon* and *Respublica* more as a characteristic of the author's style than as a versificatory factor, which is also true of *John the Evangelist.*[31] There is little alliteration in the Elizabethan interlude; except for *Common Conditions* it is a thing of the past which belongs to the halcyon years of Henry VIII., 1509-21.[32]

An historical outline of the measures encountered in the

[29] Saintsbury, i. 265-87.

[30] See p. 9; Schipper, i. 195-226.

[31] See p. 199, n. 18.

[32] The work of Lindsay provides a Scottish exception also in this.

dramas under consideration begins properly with the metre which dominates them, the light tetrameter couplet.[33] Appearing long before the first of the true interludes, from which it is absent, it constitutes the whole of the *Interludium de Clerico et Puella.* Thereafter it does not return until 1510 in *Wealth and Health,* where its proportions are very modest. The same is true of *The Four Elements,* and in *Hickscorner* it increases its strength until in the *Interlude of Youth* it makes up ninety per cent of the verses. It predominates in *Magnificence, The Pardoner and the Friar, Witty and Witless, The Four P's, John John,* and *Gentleness and Nobility,* all of which (except the first) may be considered the work of Heywood. *Godly Queen Hester,* although using this tumbling verse for filler as *Magnificence* had ten years ago, permits other and more elaborate types of versification to backwind it. Four-fifths of *Wit and Science* is in cantilever verse, which returns to reign over Heywood's last plays of *The Weather* and *Love.* Its scope is bounded on one side by 1300 and on the other by 1577, although traces of it are to be found as late as 1593 in *Summer's Last Will and Testament.*

The chief use of the tetrameter couplet is for a vehicle to bear the play onward. Not only is it useful to fill in the spaces between the more decorative forms of verse like tailrime and rime royal,[34] but it very often takes over the burden of the whole play.[35]

[33] In the *pot pourri* of Lindsay it is lost, but after 1537 *Thersites, John the Baptist, The Temptation of Our Lord, Jacob and Esau, The Nice Wanton, John Bon, Somebody and Others, The Old Man and his Wife, Jack Juggler, Respublica, John the Evangelist, Impatient Poverty, Like Will to Like, King Darius, Albion Knight, New Custom, Damon and Pythias, Enough is as Good as a Feast, Patient and Meek Grissell, The Trial of Treasure, Liberality and Prodigality, The Marriage of Wit and Science, Marriage of Wit and Wisdom,* and *All for Money* are dominated by it.

[34] As in *Godly Queen Hester, Lusty Juventus, The Old Man and his Wife, John the Evangelist, Impatient Poverty, Enough is as Good as a Feast, Patient and Meek Grissell, The Marriage of Wit and Science,* and *The Tide Tarrieth No Man.*

[35] See above, n. 33.

Particularly in the later interludes it is the metre of the vices in contrast to that of the virtuous characters who speak in rime royal[36] or septenaries.[37] The extent to which cantilever verse so often predominates over the more dignified and upright measure is often an amusing commentary on the dramatist's attention and interest. Too much, of course, must not be made of this, for no audience of the late sixteenth century would have been content with the bitter pills to purge an immoral melancholy that well had served those who attended the Morality Plays. It is hardly to be imagined that the stilted and rather wretched versifying of the complicated metres was so pleasing either to spectators or playwrights;[38] it is easy to exaggerate the pleasures of waiting to see what rime will come out next.

In contrast to the three well-defined purposes to which tetrameter couplets were set, there is the comparatively purposeless pentameter, sometimes called Alexandrine.[39] It does not differ in function from the line of four stresses to fill the spaces between rimes royal.[40] Its chronological limits are defined by *Wealth and Health* in 1510 to Nashe's interlude of 1593, in which it appears more as an interloper, blanking blank verse with rime, than as a welcome guest.[41]

The matter of hexameter couplets parallels that of pentam-

[36] *The Nice Wanton, The Cruel Debtor,* and *The Trial of Treasure.*

[37] *Cambyses* and *Appius and Virginia.*

[38] Slight variants are the substitution of pentameters or Alexandrines for tetrameters in *God's Promises.* In *The Conflict of Conscience* the lines of four beats are particularly associated with the vice scenes, and the longer lines, of seven and more stresses, go into scenes of good. In *Like Will to Like* alternate rime is the vehicle for what is good, and couplets supervene when good is in abeyance.

[39] See p. 90; not the hexapod.

[40] *God's Promises* and *King John.*

[41] Seldom does it appear as a distinct entity like a true heroic couplet of the eighteenth century. Mainly it seems to be an acromegalous form of tumbling verse, as in *The Prodigal Son* and *Albion Knight.* It is the dominating metre of few plays: *A Satire of the Three Estates, Three Laws, King John,* and *Abraham's Sacrifice.* In *The Old Man and his Wife* and *All for Money* its proportions nearly approach those of the prevailing tetrameters. In *Tom Tyler and his Wife, Respublica,* and *The Glass of Government* it serves for prologue.

eters. The first appearance is across the border in 1535 with *A Satire of the Three Estates*, a false start before 1569 in *Cambyses*, where its rôle was still small.[42] In the metrically riotous plays between 1568 and 1570[43] it occurs in little amounts, but it carries no more significance than the measures it accompanies. Throughout the interlude it was never accounted a separate metre; it grew merely by the faulty construction either of septenaries or, *mirabile dictu*, of tetrameters.

Poulter's measure[44] occurs in three plays, and in each the author paid no heed to prosody. It comes first in 1569 in *The Marriage of Wit and Science*, abides for the sake of the prologue in the *Marriage of Wit and Wisdom*, and departs with *The Glass of Government* in 1575.

Rimed septenaries date from after 1569 when they first grace the royal scenes in *Cambyses*. Thereafter they were used for the narrative parts of Livy's tale in *Appius and Virginia*, for the regal scenes of *Horestes*, the delineation of Gautier's sphere in *Patient and Meek Grissell*, for the mass of *Common Conditions*, a large part of the *Marriage of Wit and Wisdom*, for grist to Gascoigne's mill of versification, and for prologue to *The Three Ladies of London*. Its use is generally in contradistinction to that of the dramatic doggerel, which belongs to scenes of vice and frivolous activity. It lends, by virtue of nearly doubling the number of stresses, a dignity to scenes which might otherwise lack it. After 1582 they appear no longer in the interludes.

Skeltonics are as old as the interlude itself, for they are easily to be discovered in the asperities of *Fulgens and Lucres*. Traces exist in *The Four Elements, Hickscorner*, and more especially *Youth*, not to mention the cleverly rimed hemistichs of Skelton's own *Magnificence*. In the case of

[42] Either by itself or as an adjunct of poulter's measure; see pp. 8, 153; Hendren, pp. 94-6.

[43] *Liberality and Prodigality, The Marriage of Wit and Science*, and *Marriage of Wit and Wisdom*. Hexameters later recur in *The Three Ladies of London*.

[44] See p. 153, n. 3; cf. p. 133, n. 5.

Skeltonic doggerel, however, one must be careful to distinguish between hemistichic couplets and stanzaic forms whose individual lines are half-length. In *Magnificence*, for example, one finds rime royal of dipodies, composed of Skeltonics; the term is here taken in its most embracing sense, taking in not only couplets but quatrains and even, in this case, rime royal. The short lines have a tang and a zest that sits well on the vices, to whom they are usually given.[45] The limits of Skeltonics are best taken as 1512 and 1540.

The first of the interludes introduces rime couée[46] of six and eight lines, the six-line type predominating. From this time onward it is the measure of the vices or lighter element in the plays, a scheme which Medwall seconded in *Nature* and was followed until tail-rime altogether disappeared in 1576 with *The Tide Tarrieth No Man.*[47] Occasionally near the beginning of the century, in those plays whose prosody is of no significance, rime couée belongs to other characters than vices, but this is due more to the poet's weakness than to a conscious lapse of a traditional morality. From the commencement, however, it is the property of the vicious and amusing element in the drama.

The ballad measures of from four to eight lines are founded on alternate rime or quatrains.[48] They first appear in *The World and the Child*, 1509, where they have no more

[45] Skeltonics are to be found in the following interludes other than those mentioned above: *The Pardoner and the Friar, Witty and Witless, Godly Queen Hester, Wit and Science, Thersites, Three Laws, Tom Tyler, Impatient Poverty,* and *John the Evangelist.* The traces in *King Darius, Abraham's Sacrifice,* etc., are negligible.

[46] Schipper, ii. 492-518, 576-608.

[47] All *The Droichis Part of the Play* is written in tail-rime, and the vices claim it for their own in *Wealth and Health, The Four Elements, Godly Queen Hester, A Satire of the Three Estates, Three Laws, Lusty Juventus, The Old Man and his Wife, John the Evangelist,* and *Impatient Poverty.* Its last true appearance is in this play, for rime couée belongs in *Albion Knight* to song and in *The Tide Tarrieth No Man* to the induction of Courage the vice. There is perhaps an echo of its use in *Thersites*, pp. 79-80.

[48] See above, p. 8; Hendren, pp. 36-99. Schipper, ii. 479-82.

significance than the rest of the metres in the play.[49] Its last appearance to a noticeable extent is in *The Peddler's Prophecy* in 1590.

There is no consistency in its use. Usually it serves merely to vary the monotony of lines that have been riming by twos, and in *The Pardoner and the Friar* it is used for stichomythic passages. It opened *The Four P's* and was employed by characters of low degree in *The Play of the Weather*, by good characters in *Like Will to Like*, by vices in *Enough is as Good as a Feast*, and for scenes of struggle between good and evil in *The Nice Wanton*. There was, therefore, no fixed type of episode or class of character with which it, like rime couée, might be linked; and when the various playwrights did take notice of cross-rime as a separate measure, they used it in any way that was convenient for them.

The ballad-six first enters the compass of interludes at the very beginning, 1497, where in *Fulgens and Lucres* it constitutes a slight aberration from rime royal.[50] This is frequently the case;[51] at other times it is almost indistinguishable from cross-rime.[52] In *The Four Elements* it is balanced against tail-rime, the former being used for the serious passages and the latter, as usual, for the lighter episodes. In *Damon and Pythias* it makes a fleeting appearance in the dirge of Eubulus[53] and serves for prologue to *Liberality and*

[49] The same is true of *Wealth and Health, Hickscorner, Youth, John John, Wit and Science, Temperance and Humility, A Satire of the Three Estates, Thersites, The Disobedient Child, Mary Magdalene, Respublica, John the Evangelist, The Longer Thou Livest, Liberality and Prodigality, The Trial of Treasure, The Glass of Government, All for Money,* and *The Peddler's Prophecy.* That it provides the chief vehicle in four plays has already been mentioned (pp. 182-3); they are here reviewed as *The Disobedient Child, Mary Magdalene, The Longer Thou Livest,* and *The Peddler's Prophecy.*

[50] See above, p. 17, n. 8; Schipper, ii. 614-8.

[51] *Hickscorner* and *Liberality and Prodigality.*

[52] *The Disobedient Child, The Nice Wanton,* and *Like Will to Like.*

[53] See p. 134.

Prodigality; in *Patient and Meek Grissell* its purpose is to provide a verse-cart for the vices. As in the case of alternate rime, there is no steadfastness of purpose which binds all uses of the ballad-six together up to its final appearance in *All for Money*, 1577.

Rime royal is the monarch of measures.[54] A ballad stave of seven lines, it follows the Tudor interlude from its beginning through to 1590, when it rounded *The Peddler's Prophecy*. Its chief purpose, following Henry Medwall's leadership, was for passages of a serious nature.[55] Seldom is its presence without purpose,[56] but interludes are sometimes written exclusively in the Chaucerian stanza; namely, *Calisto and Melibea, Robin Conscience, God's Promises,* and *The Conflict of Conscience.*

An offshoot of this method of treatment is its assignment to characters of an exalted station, like Jupiter in *The Play of the Weather.*[57] Great persons who fall on evil days in tumbling verse, voice their grief in rime royal,[58] and they are suffered to repent in the same verse form.[59] It is but a step from this to a harangue to the audience by such characters, and this too is taken in the heptastich.[60] The revolution in prosodic application which has occurred in *Horestes* has been pointed out;[61] the exceptional allotment of the Chaucerian measure to vice is once more written down here

[54] See above, pp. 9, 122; Schipper, ii. 619-21.

[55] In *Fulgens and Lucres, Nature, Godly Queen Hester, Three Laws, God's Promises, The Nice Wanton, Enough is as Good as a Feast, Patient and Meek Grissell,* and *The Trial of Treasure.*

[56] In only *Hickscorner* and *Temperance and Humility.*

[57] Also true of the *Three Laws, The Temptation of Our Lord, King John,* and *Lusty Juventus.*

[58] In *Magnificence, The Cruel Debtor,* and *The Tide Tarrieth No Man.*

[59] Particularly in *Wealth and Health.*

[60] *Magnificence, Witty and Witless, The Play of Love, God's Promises, Lusty Juventus,* and *The Old Man and his Wife.*

[61] See pp. 136-7.

in the summary. The chief function of rime royal is in introducing and ending the interlude, acting as prologue[62] and epilogue,[63] and therein it surpasses all other measures.[64]

The history of the ballad-eight[65] begins in 1512 with John Rastell's *The Nature of the Four Elements* and is concluded in 1569 with *The Marriage of Wit and Science*. The use of the measure is akin to that of rime royal: it serves for the more sober portions of the dramas[66] and belongs to the force of good and virtue.[67] In *Hickscorner*, like the rest of the measures, it is without purpose; elsewhere it is employed for prologue[68] and epilogue,[69] all in all identical in point of treatment with the ballad-seven of *Troilus and Criseyde*.

Blank verse[70]—and prose too[71]—first enters the theatre of the interlude in *The Three Lords and Three Ladies of London* in 1588, and its coming is permanent. It is uniformly balanced against prose when the playwright is willing

[62] *The Four Elements, Godly Queen Hester, The Three Laws, God's Promises, John the Baptist, The Temptation of Our Lord, Jacob and Esau, Lusty Juventus, John Bon, Mary Magdalene, Jack Juggler, The Longer Thou Livest, Impatient Poverty, The Trial of Treasure, The Tide Tarrieth No Man, All for Money, The Three Lords and Three Ladies of London,* and *The Peddler's Prophecy.*

[63] *The Four P's, Gentleness and Nobility, Wit and Science, John the Baptist, The Temptation of Our Lord, Jacob and Esau, Jack Juggler, The Longer Thou Livest, Impatient Poverty, Cambyses, The Glass of Government, The Three Lords and Three Ladies of London.*

[64] See also p. 213.

[65] See above, p. 9; Schipper, ii. 626-7.

[66] *The Four Elements* and *A Satire of the Three Estates.*

[67] *John the Evangelist.*

[68] *The Marriage of Wit and Science.*

[69] *A Satire of the Three Estates.*

[70] Schipper, ii. 256-87, etc.; see also above, p. 201.

[71] A discussion of the prose in the interludes naturally does not deserve to be considered here; the subject has been touched in two works already cited: J. F. Macdonald, "The Use of Prose in English Drama Before Shakespeare," *University of Toronto Quarterly* (1933), ii. 465-81; and Marie Muncaster, "The Use of Prose in Elizabethan Drama," *Modern Language Review* (1919), xiv. 10-5. Since neither

to give the matter his attention,[72] and its use is to sustain the scenes and language of the respectable characters against the encroachment of villains[73] and villeins.[74] By the time that this form of poetry came to the interlude, all notion of prosodic variation had rather well been put aside, and one cannot attribute any great moment to the segregation of verse from prose.[75] It was late in the day of the Tudor interlude when blank verse arrived, a time when all sight of metrical distinction was dim, in the *crépuscule du matin.*

of these has mentioned all the interludes, a list is here appended, with the amount of prose contained:

	%
Nature:	.2
Wit and Science:	8.8
A Satire of the Three Estates:	1.8
Three Laws:	.2
The Longer Thou Livest:	.2
Damon and Pythias:	2.8
Liberality and Prodigality:	6.6
(*The Glass of Government*:	87.8)
The Three Ladies of London:	.8
The Three Lords and Three Ladies of London:	27.3
The Peddler's Prophecy:	.4
A Merry Knack to Know a Knave:	20.2
The Cobbler's Prophecy:	25.7
Summer's Last Will and Testament:	46.7

The table graphically illustrates the way in which the functions of rime were taken over by prose, and incidentally suggests that the earlier projected date of *The Peddler's Prophecy*, 1562, may be more correct than the accepted one; see above, p. 182, n. 1.

[72] Little attention is paid to the matter in *A Merry Knack to Know a Knave* and *The Cobbler's Prophecy.*

[73] *The Three Lords and Three Ladies of London.*

[74] *A Merry Knack to Know a Knave.*

[75] Shakespeare's contrasting use of prose and blank verse is in this regard interesting and quite similar.

APPENDIX A.

A Metrical Table of Prologue and Epilogues

	Prologue	*Epilogue*
Nature:	Rime royal	Rime royal
The World and the Child:	tetrameter quatrain	ballad-six
Wealth and Health:		rime royal
The Four Elements:	rime royal	(rime couée)
Hickscorner:	tetrameter quatrain	tetrameter quatrain
Magnificence:	(rime royal)	(rime royal)
John the Evangelist:	(ballad-eight)	
The Pardoner and the Friar:	tetrameter couplets	
Witty and Witless:		rime royal
The Four P's:		rime royal
Godly Queen Hester:	rime royal	
Calisto and Melibea:	(rime royal)	(rime royal)
Gentleness and Nobility:		rime royal
Wit and Science:		rime royal
The Play of Love:	(rime royal)	(rime royal)
The Play of the Weather:		rime royal
A Satire of the Three Estates:	treizain	treizain
Thersites:	rime royal	
Three Laws:	rime royal	tetrameter couplets
God's Promises:	rime royal	
John the Baptist:	rime royal	rime royal
The Temptation of Our Lord:	rime royal	rime royal
King John:	(rime royal)	(rime royal)
Jacob and Esau:	rime royal	rime royal
The Nice Wanton:	tetrameter quatrain	rime royal
John Bon:	rime royal	
Lusty Juventus:	rime royal	(rime royal)
Mary Magdalene:	rime royal	pentameter couplets
(*Roister Doister*:	rime royal	tetrameter couplets)
Tom Tyler and his Wife:	pentameter couplets	
(*Gammer Gurton's Needle*:	tetrameter couplets)	
Respublica:	pentameter couplets	
The Longer Thou Livest:	rime royal	rime royal
The Conflict of Conscience:	rime royal	heptameter rime royal
The Disobedient Child:	tetrameter quatrain	tetrameter quatrain
Like Will to Like:	ballad-six	
Jack Juggler:	rime royal	rime royal
King Darius:	tetrameter couplets	
Appius and Virginia:	heptameter couplets	heptameter couplets

New Custom:	tetrameter couplets	(tetrameter couplets)
Damon and Pythias:	heptameter couplets	
Horestes:	(rime royal)	(rime royal)
Enough is as Good as a Feast:	rime royal	ballad-six
Patient and Meek Grissell:	heptameter couplets	rime royal
The Trial of Treasure:	(rime royal)	(tetrameter couplets)
Liberality and Prodigality:	ballad-six	ballad-six
Cambyses:	heptameter couplets	rime royal
The Marriage of Wit and Science:	(ballad-eight)	
Common Conditions:	heptameter couplets	heptameter couplets
Marriage of Wit and Wisdom:	poulter's measure	heptameter couplets
Abraham's Sacrifice:	pentameter couplets	pentameter couplets
The Glass of Government:	pentameter quatrain	rime royal
The Tide Tarrieth No Man:	rime royal	(tetrameter quatrain)
All for Money:	rime royal	
The Three Ladies of London:	heptameter couplets	
The Three Lords and Three Ladies of London:	rime royal	rime royal
The Peddler's Prophecy:	rime royal	tetrameter quatrain
The Cobbler's Prophecy:	(blank verse)	(blank verse)
Summer's Last Will and Testament:	prose	prose

One observes immediately that three out of four interludes are provided with prologue and epilogue, and that half of the interludes contain both. The distribution is not uneven, but there are a few more prolegomena. From the present point of view the chief interest in them is the metre in which they are written, rime royal being predominant to a large extent. With the other ballad measures of four to eight lines, other metres are almost excluded. Rime royal was considered the proper verse for prologue and epilogue, and the cases in which this consideration is violated by couplets, of four to seven beats, are exceptional.

APPENDIX B.

A Chronological Table of Metres

1300 Inception of tetrameter couplets.
1497 Inception of rime royal, rime couée, and ballad-six.
1509 Inception of quatrains; beginning of the chief alliterative period.
1512 Inception of ballad-eight and Skeltonics.
1521 End of the chief alliterative period.
1540 End of Skeltonics.
1569 Inception of heptameter couplets, inception of poulter's measure, end of ballad-eight.
1573 End of poulter's measure.
1576 End of rime couée.
1577 End of ballad-six.
1582 End of heptameter couplets.
1588 End of rime royal; inception of blank verse and prose.
1590 End of quatrains.
1593 End of tetrameter couplets.

APPENDIX C.

(Ralph) Roister Doister[1]

Text: Adams, pp. 423-468.
Date: 1550.[2]
Rhythm: light.
Prevailing metre: tetrameter couplets.

Lines:	1908	%
Dissyllabic rime:	176	9.2
Redundant rime:	3	.2
Identical rime:	21	1.1
Latin rime:	1	.1
Rime lacking:	23	1.3
Tetrameter couplets:	1880	98.5
Tetrameter rime royal:[3]	28	1.5

Except for the four stanzas of light rime royal which serve as prologue, the entire comedy of *Ralph Roister Doister* is written in the dramatic doggerel. The verse is consistent and the rimes are good.[4] The epilogue[5] is not differentiated prosodically from the last scene of the fifth act which precedes it, but continues in the same tumbling verse which Matthew Merry-Greek inaugurated at the opening of Act I. Rime lapses most particularly in the episodes in which Ralph speaks with Madge Mumblecrust of his marriage plans,[6] and when the bells peal at the ringing of the parish clerk and Ralph's henchmen.[7] The verse also suffers perceptibly in the episode of the letter,[8] which is twice read; the rime is kept up, but variation from the strict couplet is quite noticeable.

[1] Bradner, pp. 379-80; Reyher, p. 60; Saintsbury, i. 337; Schipper, i. 234.

[2] Eckhardt, i. 59.

[3] Prologue.

[4] Little/mickle (II. i. 7/8), mome/none (V. ii. 27/8), open/spoken (V. iii. 3/4).

[5] Text, p. 468.

[6] I. iii. 133-139.

[7] III. iii. 83-85, 90-94.

[8] III. iv. 36-96; v. 49-83.

Prosodic variety is thus seen to be confined to the prologue. Once this is spoken, the verse settles into the lines of four stresses, and nothing then budges it. Nicholas Udall must therefore be considered as not interested in changing his verse to accord with the action that occurs or with the characters who speak the verse. He bowed sufficiently to tradition in writing the Chaucerian stanzas for the prologue, but thence he kept to the dramatic metre of tumbling verse.

APPENDIX D.

GAMMER GURTON'S NEEDLE[1]

Text: Adams, pp. 469-499.
Date: 1553.[2]
Rhythm: very light.
Alliteration: sparing.
Prevailing metre: tetrameter couplets.[3]

Lines:	1247	%
Dissyllabic rime:	226	18.1
Identical rime:	1	..
Redundant rime:	1	..
Internal rime:[4]	6	.5
Rime lacking:	3	.2
Tetrameter couplets:[3]	1119	89.7
Trimeter sixain coué:	54	4.3
Dimeter couplets:	27	2.2
Dimeter quatrain:[5]	24	1.9
Dimeter sixain coué:[6]	10	.8
Tetrameter rime royal:	7	.6
Tetrameter quatrain:	4	.3
Monometer dizain coué:[4]	2	.2

"Gammer Gurtons Nedle" is written in the long straggling measure, dramatic doggerel couplets of uncertain length.[3] The rimes are of moderate quality.[7] A rare effect is achieved

[1] Bond, pp. lxxxii, lxxxvi; Bradner, p. 379; Reyher, p. 60; Saintsbury, i. 337.

[2] Text, p. 469.

[3] Immiscible with poulter's measure. There are also eight lines of leash where the second and third scenes of the fourth act are joined.

[4] Two lines (III. iii. 25-26) have the rime composition aabbc ddeec; to illustrate their rime couée they should be printed as ten.

[5] Each of these lines (IV. ii. 5-28) is terminated by an ejaculatory "see now?"

[6] The four lines in III. iii. 21-24 ought to be set up as six to show their rime couée.

[7] Making/taken (I. v. 27/8), within it/find it (50/1). Some of the worst of the rimes are to be found in III. ii. 1-6, and for purposes of rime a metathetic *r* exists in burst thee/crust thee (V. ii. 96/7: it may be a printer's error); see p. 153, n. 7.

by the heaviness of the couplets in which Doctor Rat bemoans the kitchen beating he has received at the hands of Dame Chat and her maids.[8] Accentually, however, the verse remains a bog; once again each line must be scanned separately, and scansion merely illustrates that poulter's measure cannot always be distinguished from couplets whose number of accents is continually varying. As in the case of *John the Evangelist,* one cannot tell whether a line has four, five, six, or seven ictus, and the syllabication continues wretched throughout.[9]

The comedy is begun and ended with the tumescent tetrameters; prologue[10] and epilogue[11] are not metrically distinct from the hulk of the play. Rime royal makes its only intrusion at the beginning of the last scene when the "Bayly" starts to adjudicate the squabble between the Doctor and Dame Chat.[12] One strophe, however, exhausts the dramaturgical facility, and the Bayly is required to slip back into couplets. Cross-rime appears when Dame Chat begins to resent Doctor Rat's forensic evidence and inserts a line or two alternately,[13] but the display of his broken head suffices to restore immediate rime. William Stevenson, the accepted author, had tried out alternate rime before,[14] but his purpose had been different: Hodge, the eager *scurra,* had been breathlessly trying to explain the fate of the "neele" to the Doctor.

Rime doggerel, like the ballad measures, is of little import

[8] IV. iv. 45-48. "Woe worth the day that I came here . . ." is a satirically iambic indictment of the language of lamentation; one compares this with the seriousness of its treatment in *Damon and Pythias,* text, p. 602. As Doctor Rat begins to feel better, the verse gathers speed; and by the time he has made up his mind for immediate revenge, the verse hurries off with him.

[9] This is nowhere closer to the truth than in the tail-rime of III. iii. 21-26.

[10] Text, p. 470.

[11] Text, p. 499.

[12] V. ii. 1-7.

[13] So that her interruptions, like her remarks, if viewed consecutively and separately, are really couplets. This will recall the same method of treatment in *The Pardoner and the Friar,* pp. 43-4.

[14] In dimeter: IV. ii. 5-28; see n. 5.

as it makes its way experimentally into the play. Its sole appearance[15] is to be found near the commencement: Diccon the Bedlam, his poor wits more addled than ever by having visited Dame Chat's ale-house, dominates a brief passage of low comedy with Hodge "breechelesse." Diccon's verse is good rime couée and relatively far superior to the doggerel couplets of the law and the ministry.

Serious inroads are therefore never made into the plain dramatic doggerel by ballad systems or tail-rime. A specimen of rime couée in a portion presided over by the "rechelesse" Diccon provides a nostalgic *soupçon* of the vice-scenes, mainstays of the pre-Elizabethan interlude; a quatrain speaks from the days of John Heywood to heighten altercation: *sed magnum est distichon et praevalet.*

[15] II. i. 17-ii. 18; the pairs of couplets noted above (nn. 4, 5) are merely tricked out with the semblance of rime couée, specious *infioriture.* They belong to the rapid passage at arms between Dame Chat and Gammer Gurton in which the logomachy achieves its climax. Cf. p. 160.

APPENDIX E.

King Ahasuerus and Queen Hester

Text: W. W. Greg, ed., *Materialen zur Kunde des älteren englischen Dramas* (Louvain, 1904), v. pp. xv-xvi.
Date: 1600.[1]
Rhythm: heavy.
Prevailing metre: pentameter couplets.

Lines:	46	%
Rime lacking:	2	4.3
Pentameter couplets:	46	100.

This late interlude, printed by Greg with *Godly Queen Hester,* has attracted very little critical attention, and there is not much to speak of with regard to its prosody. The verse is good heroic couplets, and we can only note the change to five iambic feet. Since there is no alteration in the author's treatment of the metre, it cannot be held that he considered it worthy of variation, and over its unworthiness we are able to pass rapidly.

[1] J. J. Elson, ed., *The Wits, or Sport upon Sport* (Ithaca [N. Y.], 1932), pp. 406-7.

INDEX